Confidence Unchained!

The 5 Practices for Releasing Self-Doubt and Living Confidently

Vicki Haddock

Copyright © 2023 Vicki Haddock

All rights reserved.

ISBN: 9798371627162

DEDICATION

This book is dedicated to the three humans who chose to travel with me as their mom in this lifetime. You were the catalysts for my personal growth journey. I was determined to role model a new way for you – and in the process I found me.

All my love to the moon and back.

Introduction _____ *1*

Chapter 1 - Understanding Where Self-Doubt Originates _____ *5*

    5 Sources of Conditioning _____ 7

    Questions You May Ask along the Way (And It's Okay) _____ 13

    3 Mental Shifts to Support Finding Your True Value _____ 14

Chapter 2 - Rewiring your Brain for Change _____ *17*

    KEY 1 - Confidence-Building Statements _____ 18

    New Perspective = New Results _____ 21

Chapter 3 - Creating consistent connection _____ *25*

    Key Practice 2 - Listening to Heart-Centered Intuitive Guidance 26

    New Perspective = New Results _____ 32

Chapter 4 - Be Guided by a Clear Vision of the Future _____ *35*

    Key Practice 3 - Clarity _____ 36

    Creating a New Map of Reality _____ 39

    New Perspective = New Results _____ 43

Chapter 5 - Confident Communication _____ *47*

    Key Practice 4 – Developing the Skill of Confident Communication _____ 48

    New Perspective = New Results _____ 57

Chapter 6 - Give Yourself a Break _____ *61*

    Key Practice 5 - Compassion _____ 62

    New Perspective = New Results _____ 64

Chapter 7 - Living the 5 Key Practices: Living Life to the Fullest _____ *69*

    The 5 Confidence-Building Key Practices: Adapt and Support You as You Grow _____ 70

ACKNOWLEDGMENTS

I would like to take a moment to acknowledge a few people who have been key parts of my transformational journey and the creation of this book. First of all, thank you to the teachers who came before me that were willing to let their light shine for others: especially Wayne Dyer, Eckhart Tolle, and Michael Singer. To those who have traveled the road personally with me – thank you my dear friend Janet, the numerous coaches who facilitated my growth, and so many others who encouraged me along the way! I want to extend another very special thank you to those who gave permission for me to share their personal stories here. Their stories bring to life the concepts I share and prove change is possible!

Thank you also to those who had a hand in polishing this book and making it easier to read. Thank you especially to Charlotte Lang who edited, encouraged, and simplified the manuscript.

I acknowledge you – the reader – for being open to inviting transformation into your life. Let the journey begin!

INTRODUCTION

"Happiness and self-confidence come naturally when you feel yourself moving and progressing toward becoming the very best person that you can be."
— Brian Tracy

Self-Doubt.

That nagging voice inside your head keeps you walking on eggshells and playing it safe, separating you from the desires hiding in your heart. Your destiny shrinks inside you like a shadow. A faint drumbeat you know is there yet feels unreachable. You know you were created for so much more than this. But how? "How?" is the excuse we use to remain small. "I don't know HOW I could make that happen." Our dreams exist on the other side of this chasm of self-doubt.

The canyon of doubt feels dangerous and risky when there is no visible bridge between where you are and the confident, fulfilling life you desire to live. Questions fill your mind like unwanted voices mocking your silent dreams. The unspoken truth is that you're not sure you can...or even deserve... to live a fulfilling, happy life.

You are not alone. In fact, if your eyes could see all the self-doubt those around you walk with every day, you would realize you have plenty of company. Self-doubt keeps us stuck in relationships, jobs, and geographical locations that leave us feeling like we are merely surviving instead of thriving. From the faithful employee who silently can't stand her job anymore, an entrepreneur taking the next leap to start a business, or a mom questioning how to parent her teenager, they all have self-doubt in common. Some of the most outwardly confident individuals I know will openly share their battles of self-doubt during moments of authenticity. Our busy culture gives us an easy out. It's easier to be busy "doing" something than to slow down long enough to look at our inner doubt.

I would know. This used to be me!

Discovering my own self-confidence and value are the keys that unlocked my life and shifted it from barely surviving to thriving. Today I've used these same keys to help hundreds of clients leave behind self-doubt and claim a thriving life. I will teach you the five key practices that led me to the thriving life I have today. I'm writing in a cute coffee shop near the ocean right now and loving life completely. Without these five key practices, I'm sure I would still be just surviving.

I remember the day I realized finding my own inner confidence was no longer optional. Life circumstances were squeezing me to the point of extreme misery. I've heard it said that you have to hit rock bottom before you find your way back up. I discovered these key practices while recovering from my rock-bottom experiences.

I vividly remember that morning years ago: My alarm nagged at me to get up. Even after a "full night's sleep," I barely had the energy to hit the snooze button, precisely calculating the shortest number of minutes I needed to get my kids out of bed, fed, and out the door to school. My insides felt on fire with misery, and all I wanted to do was pull the covers back over my head and never face the world again.

I swirled dizzily in a hurricane of self-doubt as I laid there in bed that early morning. My mind spun even faster than my normal monkey mind of swirling thoughts.

My thoughts were consumed with doubt. I blamed myself for the demise of my marriage, my uncertainty at work, and I felt like I was ruining my children's lives. How had I screwed things up so badly? The list of self-doubts and judgments raged inside my head:

I didn't do enough.

It's my fault.

I should have seen it sooner.

Why can't I just be happy?

Am I capable of being happy?

Can I actually create a different life? Maybe I'm too messed up.

Is this thing called inner peace even real?

There has to be more to life than this; maybe I'll never find it.

I deserve this misery.

Somewhere in that hurricane of self-doubt, I decided I would NOT live the next 20 years of my life this way.

I became determined to break the family patterns of addiction, suffering, misery, and overhelping that had led my relationship to collapse. That day, I committed to searching until I found the answers that would break the invisible chains that kept me living in silence. I would find my way and my voice, and role model a new way for my children. That day, the pain of change became less than the pain of remaining the same. My decision to demand change set in motion a life-changing learning journey.

That commitment led me on a journey where I discovered the five key confidence-building practices that saved my life. They became the bridge over the deep chasm of self-doubt.

Here is what I discovered: Self-doubt is the primary obstacle standing between you and your heart's desires. It is possible to transcend self-doubt when you commit to a new future. The first step in creating that new future begins with understanding the origins of your self-doubt.

Radical healing is yours when you learn and integrate these confidence-building practices into your daily life. With these practices, you'll be equipped to break old cycles and patterns and finally experience the fulfilling life you were always meant to live.

CHAPTER 1 - UNDERSTANDING WHERE SELF-DOUBT ORIGINATES

"Your unhappiness ultimately arises not from the circumstances of your life but from the conditioning of your mind."
— *Eckhart Tolle*

The first step in transcending self-doubt begins with understanding its origins. Self-doubt constantly lived in my brain. Trying to get rid of it felt like rejecting myself. The doubts seemed so real that they felt like my identity -- part of my personality. Letting go of self-doubt became easier when I finally found the reason why the thoughts existed. I began to realize the thoughts of self-doubt were not ME, but instead collective voices from my past conditioning. Most importantly, I realized I could choose whether I wanted to listen to them. I had the choice to rise above or transcend them!

Let's take a peek at the word 'transcend.' I chose this word as a way of describing how we rise above doubt in our lives. I am not going to promise that you will eliminate self-doubt altogether. As you grow to new levels in your life and explore new layers of learning, you will also encounter variations of self-doubt. Yet, once you recognize them for the illusion they are. It will be easier to recognize the same old self-doubt no matter what disguise it appears in. Then, you are prepared to shift your attention away from this illusion and to the truth of your brilliance and creativity.

Transcending is similar to comparing your life to a high-rise building. You currently live on floor one with all of these furnishings called doubt, fear, and anxiety. They seem comfortable and familiar because you know them so well, but one day you discover an elevator that takes you to floor two. Floor two is decorated in an entirely different style. It feels hopeful, lighter, yet new and unfamiliar and a little uncomfortable. Floor one, with all its doubt furnishings, is still there, and if you choose to hop in the elevator and go down, you will back amidst all your familiar doubts. Instead, think of these five practices as the elevator to help you explore all of the amazing levels of potential that already exist inside of you - they just need to be discovered!

Let's go back to the origin of doubts and take a closer look. We begin by rewinding the clock back to the day you were born. You arrived into this world as an innocent, beautiful baby full of trust and possibility: a bundle of pure potential.

This innocent, whole, worthy, beautiful spirit of pure potential is who you truly are. If we all were raised in environments that encouraged self-discovery and cultivated personal strengths there would be no need for a book on self-doubt. The majority of us instead experience growing up in environments where shortcomings gained more attention than strengths which were not cultivated.

Our caretakers molded and influenced us based on their own limited perceptions of themselves and how they were raised. Often the focus was on deficiencies, following rules, and conforming to community norms. Or, for others, the complete absence of any structure or attention resulting in neglect. These experiences act like layers of dirt and grime gathering on window glass. Eventually, the view through the glass becomes marred. The original view is completely forgotten, and instead, it seems as if the distorted view is all there ever was.

As I've cleared the layers of filth that obscured my view and helped others to do the same, I've discovered five primary ways the view becomes distorted through how we were conditioned. We will take a look at them next.

5 Sources of Conditioning

> *"What gets in our way is history and culture and religion and economic conditions. It is part of the hypnosis of our social conditioning."*
> — Deepak Chopra

The first seven years of a child's life are the most significant for learning and development. Throughout these first seven years, a child has no filter for right/wrong, good/bad, or healthy/unhealthy. Everything experienced is accepted as truth without question. During these formative years, a child takes on the values, norms, and expectations of the culture and family in which they are raised. Let's look at how this happens.

Take a moment to think about a baby that has been special to you. Maybe your own child, a niece or nephew, or a friend's child. Imagine that baby within the first six months of their life. As you hold the baby's face in your mind's eye (maybe he is laughing or she is quietly sleeping), ask yourself:

What is possible for this baby?

How complete is your love of this child?

How completely do you accept the baby exactly as it is?

In that moment, there is no doubt about the baby's essence and pure possibility, only complete confidence in this baby's potential. This is the essence of who each of us are – pure potential, innocence, and love, worthy of anything and everything.

What changes between the birth of the confident child and the resulting adult life riddled with self-doubt? Doubt comes from layers and layers of conditioning taught us by our experiences with others. When we take a closer look at these layers, it is easy to see how each layer has disconnected us from the reality of who we truly are and has silenced our voices.

These layers are sorted into the following five categories:
- Trauma
- Religion
- Culture
- Family Patterns
- Self-Generated Doubt

Let's take a deeper look at each of these five ways conditioning and distortion happen.

Trauma (Heightened Emotional Response)

What is trauma? One straightforward definition is an intense emotional response to an event. Trauma can refer to the aftermath of a single catastrophic accident or the repeated abuse and neglect of a person. However, it can also be as simple as your mom forgetting to pick you up from school. If your mom had a history of always picking you up on time, and then one day she lost track of time and missed getting you from practice, this could cause an intense emotional response.

Heightened emotional response or trauma, whether caused by a seemingly insignificant event or repeated abuse over time, create patterns that lead to self-doubt. The roots of the doubt lie in actual events that happened. The problem arises not with the trauma itself but the behavior that follows. A person impacted by a traumatic emotional response now begins to perceive other normal happenings in the world through the lens of that trauma. Anything with an element of similarity triggers the wound of the trauma.

Traumatic emotional responses come in many different forms. These responses layer on top of each other, often creating a false or conditioned personal identity.

The following story illustrates how trauma arises: Emily is 13, an awkward stage for many children as they shift from childhood into adolescence. Today, she is sitting at her desk at school looking at her test score. Her teacher towers over her, scolding her about how she has failed the exam and not lived up to her potential. He tells her that if she doesn't "get serious about her studies," she will never be successful. That night at home, Emily's parents reinforce the idea that she messed up, screwed up, and most likely will never live up to her potential.

Internally, Emily feels a high level of shame and guilt and feels like she can never measure up. A layer of conditioning has been placed upon Emily. It's not who she is, but the seemingly small trauma of failing the test has become a distorted lens through which she now views herself.

The next time she sits down for a test, she has images of her teacher and parents reminding her of what a failure she is as a student. These images become the subconscious operating system that now impact her actions. She now internally identifies herself as a failure.

Trauma, whether quiet or overt, becomes a shifting point. It's a point where the innocent child unknowingly puts on a distorted set of glasses and now interprets everything, including how they define themselves, through the lens of the trauma.

It was my fault.

I should have known better.

I caused it.

I didn't work hard enough.

The trauma lens distorts. It hides. It masks the authentic you and it becomes the gap in which self-doubt arises. One clear sign that trauma may be impacting your perception of yourself is when you are frustrated and stuck, you continuously spin your wheels instead of making progress. It's possible you take massive action towards a goal, but that progress is quickly lost or wiped away leaving you where you started. Until the trauma is healed and released, your subconscious will draw you back to the deceptive "safe" place again and again.

Religion

Each major religion has formed traditions, expectations, and values by which it operates. When a child grows up in a society influenced by religious teaching, that child, without even consciously knowing it, takes on the traditions, expectations, and values of that religion as if they were their own. This adds another layer of distortion that further disconnects an individual from the pure potential at their core.

There are varying degrees to which religion impacts our life. The experiences that leave the greatest negative imprint on us are those that use the name of God (or any other word for the same) to control and manipulate. (Just as a note, it does not have to be a religion but any organization that insists its message is more important than individuals and seeks to cultivate people who follow loyally without valuing individualism or independent thinking.) I personally have experienced this from a church, a multi-level marketing company, a political party, and a gifted teacher.

I grew up in an extremely fundamental religious group that planted all sorts of doubt in my mind about my worthiness and my role as a female. The experience left me with enormous amounts of guilt, shame, and fear of the consequences for not following the rules created by those in authority.

The damage of spiritual abuse is one of the worst forms of trauma because it pits you against God and those who claim to have spiritual insight greater than your own. My experience is an extreme example; however, you do not have to look far to see how similar, or even identical themes, are deeply entrenched in our culture.

Many women carry shame about their bodies and sexuality that has deep roots in the story of Adam and Eve from the Bible. Young females raised in a home where this story is told immediately receive the, perhaps unintentional, message that females are the source of men's problems and that the female body is shameful.

Whether you hold this story as truth, fable, or metaphor it's a very simple demonstration of how religious concepts can deeply drive a wedge between that innocent soul you were born as and the beliefs and values that were put on you.

What conclusion does an innocent mind reach when this repeated story is imprinted on her mind? She learns that only men are worthy to lead and that she will be responsible for what goes wrong in a man's life. Take a moment to pause and consider how religion has influenced your life.

All major religions have a central message of love and purity. Hurt results when rules, regulations, and expectations define how that love is accessed. It's critical as an independent thinker to ask whether core religious teachings and concepts align and promote love or whether they cause division, separation, and conflict. The latter is an indication that human egos, rather than the divine, are in control.

Many cultures have been built upon fundamental religious concepts that layer even more distortion and disconnection on all those who grow up within them. Religion can be part of that overall culture but culture, in general, extends even broader.

Culture

The culture in which a child is raised sets the boundaries of what the child believes is possible. Culture is made of elements of religion, family dynamics, and education, but extends to include the environment, institutional values, and societal biases. How much a culture respects women, the elderly, and each other becomes a subconscious role model to its children.

Just a few years before I was born in 1973, women were not allowed to do the following things in the United States:
- Get a bank account or a credit in her own name.
- Be guaranteed that they will not be fired for pregnancy.
- Fight on the front lines in the military.
- Obtain an Ivy League education.
- Take legal action against workplace sexual harassment.
- Decide not to have sex with her husband.

My mother was raised in an era where the main career options for a woman were secretary, nurse, or teacher. Even though I graduated from high school first in my class and could have obtained a scholarship to any school I desired, guess what advice my mom gave me?

"Do the school secretary internship so you can get a good job." Because I was raised with overlapping beliefs about religion, culture, and family, the lens I saw through made the internship acceptable, even though I was disappointed to step off the college prep path my peers were on.

Our culture in the United States has shifted so that many young girls are stepping bravely into their future. Still, when the authentic inner spark inside you is calling you to something different than what culture suggests, the self-doubt can still be intense!

Eventually, I became the first female district manager in the Midwest for an environmental waste company. Even though my business qualifications far exceeded some of my male counterparts, I had to constantly prove myself to skeptical individuals who struggled to accept a female in a male-dominated industry.

The culture of many North Americans includes an emphasis on having a "strong work ethic," but that work ethic has turned into a work addiction. This impacts family leave policies, steals times from home life, and re-enforces the idea that money and materialism are more important than the health and well-being of yourself and your family.

Our world is full of individuals who carry invisible wounds and scars inflicted by cultural norms of all types. Take a moment to pause and consider how you may have experienced cultural conditioning.

Family Patterns

Family patterns, whether healthy or unhealthy, are strongly woven into the fabric of each generation, linking each one to the next, perpetuating cycles. When patterns are healthy, they encourage ever-increasing family health. When families are toxic, they act like poison for future generations until a family member has the courage to break the cycle.

For this conversation, I am referring to harmful cycles such as addiction, overhelping, and control. Anything that a child observes, experiences, or hears from ages 0 to 7 becomes their primary pattern of operation. Children have no ability to discern at this early age, so everything they experience is taken as truth. The behaviors a child observes from their guardians during this stage become the dominant map for their future behavior.

Any behavior, communication style, or emotion that caretakers exhibit can be passed down from one generation to the next. It becomes the dominant "behavior" pattern that a child learns. To connect back to your authentic nature, you have to distinguish the family patterns and cycles placed on you after birth. Again, these patterns are not inherent to you; they belong to the family and environment in which you were raised creating layers distorting the view of yourself.

Often personal and spiritual growth work is referred to as the peeling back the layers of an onion. It's the work you do when you identify family patterns and generational trauma. Some patterns, such as addiction, whether alcoholism or over-eating, are easy to spot. Others, such as self-criticism, guilt, fear, or how you interact with your spouse, are less easy to recognize and can seem so much a part of your nature that it's difficult to distinguish the difference between a family pattern and your personality.

My great-grandfather was an angry, abusive man. My grandfather repeated that cycle with his kids, and my father endured the abuse at the hand of his father. My father had the wisdom and self-awareness to see that he had a choice to pass along the anger and harshness to his kids or break the cycle. Thankfully, he chose to break the cycle. It wasn't always easy; at times I could see he wrestled with that old conditioned nature, yet he continually chose differently and created a new opportunity for me to live free of the generational cycle of abuse.

Author Joe Dispenza is well-known for saying that our personality is shaped by our personal reality. There is much truth to this. Our personality may have formed around coping mechanisms that we needed to keep us safe and secure as a child, and those mechanisms become so much a part of our habitual way of life that they eventually seem synonymous with who we are. Peeling back the layers around family conditioning allows you to separate what part of your personality is conditioned response and what part is authentically you.

Self-Generated Doubt

You may be asking, "How can self-doubt be on a list of five things that

CAUSE self-doubt?" I left it for last on purpose, even though it may be the most significant one on the list. Here's why: Trauma, Religion, Culture, and Family Patterns are layered onto us. They are the experiences, values, norms, and expectations externally placed on us when we were too young to have the freedom to choose what influences us.

Imagine these norms and expectations as a yardstick to measure life by. The yard stick is made up of the collective expectations of your family, religion, culture, and community. Life becomes about trying to measure up to this yardstick. Self-doubt emerges between the yardstick and the values and expectations we hold deeply as true and authentic for ourselves.

Few people are good at understanding their personal values and self-expectations. It's just not a skill that is prioritized or taught. But once we recognize our internal values, that which is truly important to us as individuals, it becomes clear that self-doubt emerges in the gap between those values and societies' "measuring stick" that can never be achieved.

Your life is being unconsciously driven and conditioned by so many external sources, but this also means it's possible to shift inward, connect with our internal values, and begin to live life from a centered stable place.

Shifting to internal motivation versus external motivation releases the self-doubt that naturally arises when one attempts to act according to someone else's values, norms, and expectations. (For further guidance on how to determine your personal values, please visit my website www.vickihaddock.com and download the Discovering your Values free resource.)

Questions You May Ask along the Way (And It's Okay)

As we embark on this journey together to rediscover the greatness of who you already are, there are some common questions that surface.

Am I worth it?

Do I deserve it?

Can I actually do it?

What if I'm too broken?

Am I really enough?

Is it really possible?

Is it too late?

You are not alone in asking these questions: I've asked them, and so has every individual I have guided toward authentic self-connection and confidence. Here is what I can tell you: the reason we ask these questions is because of that same conditioning and external influences that have clung to us on our journey.

Return to that image of the brand-new baby. Would you have asked any of these questions of that baby? No! It's easy to see the pure potential of their brand-new life. We ask these questions only when the layers of conditioning and societal expectations disconnect us from our innocence and the purity of our souls.

I won't try to convince you that there are positive answers to these questions; instead, I'll promise that if you choose you and choose to embrace the five key practices that follow, you will begin to peel back the layers of distortion and reveal the true answers. One day you will realize that these questions are just more conditioned layers weighing you down, and you will then return to what you have known all along:

I am worthy (and I was never unworthy!)

I deserve everything I desire (and you always have!)

I can do it (when you trust your inner guide!)

I am whole (and the idea I was ever broken was false!)

I am enough (because I exist and was born enough)

It's never too late (as long as you have breath, change is possible)

I invite you to consider three simple perspective shifts that will make the journey of letting go of these layers of conditioning and old perspectives gentler and simpler.

3 Mental Shifts to Support Finding Your True Value

Throughout this journey, there are three key shifts I'm going to ask you to make. These shifts are like taking off the old, dirty, distorted lenses and putting on crystal-clear glasses that bring everything into focus.

1. Shift from listening to your head to listening to your heart
2. Shift from others' values to your own
3. Shift from viewing yourself as broken to viewing yourself as whole

The first shift I invite you to make is leaving the egoic headspace and embracing the authenticity of your heart. We get to choose whether to live from our analytical mind or from the soft, quiet guiding of the heart. The head is always questioning, judging, analyzing, and casting doubt. The head is loud, fast, and constantly shifting and changing. We describe it as "the voice/s in our head."

The heart space is the receiver of our intuition and sharer of our truth. We will talk more about connecting to this space in the five practices. For now, let's note that communication coming from the heart (sometimes referred to as the gut) looks and feels much different. Heart-centered communication is quiet. It is always loving, supportive, and kind. It is encouraging, certain, wise, and solid in its guidance. I often refer to this as the "eyes" of your soul. Your intuitive eyes can see forward to infinity and clearly know what's best for you at this moment, even when it does not make sense to the logical brain.

The next key shift I'll ask you to be aware of is your values. Most likely your current operating system is full of other people's values. Parents, teachers, religion, friends, governments, and countries each have unique sets of values that you have been exposed to throughout your life. It's unlikely you are clear on what your individual values are unless you've done some deep work in this area. Begin to be curious about whose values you are using as a measuring stick and seek to understand your individual values.

Every conflict in life can be traced back to a personal value. The source of conflict is confusing when we are not clear on our personal values. Becoming clear on your unique individual values helps you to see the root of the conflict. Friction happens when your values clash with the values of those around you.

A recent client of mine was having a difficult time staying engaged and motivated at his job. He kept saying he felt like he "lost his seat at the table." When we dug deep into his values, he realized that contribution and connection are two of his top five values. They added value and meaning to his job. His current role had shifted, and he no longer had the opportunity to engage in the types of connections that facilitated the feeling that he was contributing his best. Understanding this helped him discover the source of his unhappiness. Now he could easily see he had a choice to find new opportunities outside of work to fulfill that need for connection and contribution, or he could search for a new role that fit his values and strengths better.

The third shift I'm inviting you to make is to begin viewing yourself as capable, whole, and resourceful. Connect back to that image of you as a tiny baby. You were born whole and full of possibility. Conditioning and emotional wounds disconnect you temporarily from the truth of your wholeness. Now that you know, begin to step back into that image of who you always have been. So, I'm inviting you to begin viewing yourself as someone who holds all the answers you seek and can do what is needed to be confident.

These three perspective shifts will support you in the days ahead as you learn and implement the five key confidence-building practices.

This is a judgment-free process. It may be tempting when you have new "ah-ha!" moments to jump straight to self-criticism. I've spent enough time there myself to know the place well. Self-judgment serves no purpose. We do the best we can with the information we have. We know and realize things when we are meant to. We gain new awareness when we can act upon that awareness and not a moment sooner. Unawareness keeps us safe when we are not ready for new knowledge. So, if you are tempted, like I was, to go down the road of self-judgment, remember these words: Be kind to yourself. The only helpful path is forward.

Looking back, I can already see that I followed my intuition and internal guidance long before I knew what that meant. It's how I came to these five confidence-building practices. I'm sure you will recognize similarities to what you have seen or heard recommended by other experts. I learned the fundamentals of confidence-building from various respected authors, teachers, and coaches. I have taken those fundamentals, added to them from my own experience, and created five key confidence-building practices that brought me freedom. You can grow your confidence to ever-increasing new levels by making these three shifts: Begin to listen to your heart, discover your personal values, and view yourself as whole, capable, and resourceful. Releasing self-doubt is the biggest gift you can give yourself.

It's time to learn the practices that will help you rise above self-doubt and re-write your history. You get to be the maverick that breaks the generational patterns in only one generation and rewrites the future. Are you ready?

CHAPTER 2 - REWIRING YOUR BRAIN FOR CHANGE

"We perceive reality based on how our brain is wired. You can change your brain just by thinking differently."
— *Joe Dispenza*

"Neurons that fire together wire together. You can rewire your brain for higher consciousness by focusing on love."
— *Deepak Chopra*

KEY 1 - Confidence-Building Statements

What are Confidence-Building Statements?

I was determined to create change in my life. Yet daily, I began to recognize that my mind raced with thoughts that cast doubt on what was possible and made me question myself constantly. In fact, I didn't even really know who I was. Did I like eggs? Was I good at my job? Could I truly create the change I wanted to? I experienced one doubtful thought after another, and the only thing that kept me moving forward was the profound feeling that I had been born for more than this. I held onto this deep and growing sense that I had a greater mission to fulfill on this earth. I held on even when there was only a faint idea of what that purpose might be. One thing I knew for sure: I couldn't accomplish any purpose in the fearful, doubtful state I was living in.

I learned about affirmations in this season of my life. You most likely have heard of them too. Maybe you have even used them unsuccessfully or with intermittent success. What I'm about to share with you is the next-level version of affirmations that work when you work them.

Affirmations are short statements that replace an unhelpful belief or self-talk. The statements reflect the more effective belief you are choosing in your life. Affirmations have little impact if they are not believable and must be repeated long enough to become your new go-to statements. That is why I choose to call this upgraded version of affirmations "Confidence-Building Statements." Those who claim affirmations have little impact are usually missing the believability piece of the affirmation equation which we will cover shortly. Let's look at the key factors of using confidence-building statements successfully.

It takes approximately seven positives to unwire one negative. How many times have you called yourself dumb or questioned your ability to make good decisions? Now multiply that number by 7. This is the approximate number of repetitions that will unwire those negative thoughts! I bet you are already choosing your self-talk with more care!

Your current conditioned thinking patterns have been ingrained in your brain with repetition. Consider how many times a day you have practiced similar thought patterns! New thinking patterns take time to wear equally deep or deeper grooves into your brain. While you practice new thinking patterns, the previous grooves begin to weaken and diminish. Eventually, they recede into shadow.

Your brain needs an element of believability for anything you tell it. This is why affirmations like "I have a million dollars in my bank account," don't work. Your brain isn't stupid...it knows the balance of your bank account! A more believable affirmation would be: Each day the balance of my bank account grows as I make better financial choices. Your brain can imagine you making a better choice and seeing your bank account grow by $1 or $100!

Instead of shifting your thinking by leaps, try shifting it step by step. Once a confidence-building statement feels completely true, modify it slightly to continue to grow.

What do Confidence-Building Statements replace?

Confidence-building statements are used to replace the ongoing negative self-talk that happens in our heads. Those conditioned voices in your head represent a collection of people: your mother, your dad, your mean first-grade teacher, and your nasty first boss. Maybe even your ex-partner who had constantly put you down. When the brain hears a statement often enough, it is conditioned to believe it is true. It even scans the environment for proof that it is true and diminishes any reality that might confirm otherwise. Confidence-building statements are your greatest key to rewiring your brain. They allow you to choose intentionally what you say to yourself.

Where do you begin designing your own statements? Listen to what is happening inside your head. Practice self-awareness of your thoughts. Each time negative sh!t goes down in your thinking, there is an opportunity to replace the thought with a confidence-building statement. Here is the art of how to create them.

Daily Practice - How to Create and Use Confidence-Building Statements

Begin paying attention to the voice in your head. Listen to what it says. Is it helpful, or is it criticizing you and verbally punching you in the gut? It's those self-criticizing words we want to pay attention to. They tell us where to start creating solid statements that will shift our thinking.

Here is a favorite example from my own experience that many people resonate with. Self-criticizing thought: I must explain myself or others will think I'm wrong/stupid/crazy. If I can convince them of why I made the decision, everything will be ok.

I always felt like I had to explain and justify all of my decisions to everyone around me to keep them happy. Then one day, I realized that justifying my choices and actions is a co-dependent characteristic that kept me walking on eggshells.

I created the confidence-building statement: I am not obligated to justify myself. I wrote it on a notecard and read it every time I had a free moment. I read it as many times as possible; in line at the grocery store, waiting in the doctor's office, when I took a break at work, and before I went to bed. I was serious about that 7x repetition to offset one negative. I began to notice that I was responding to situations differently. Instead of jumping to explain myself, I began slowing down and more confidently owning my thoughts, beliefs, and opinions.

Here is the key to creating statements: they have to reflect an optimal outcome AND be believable. I recently helped a client craft an affirmation around health and exercise. She wanted to be more motivated to work out. Here is how the affirmation unfolded:

Self-criticizing thought: I am so unmotivated to work out, but I *should* be going to the gym every day. I'm so lazy. I deserve to be fat. (HINT: thinking the word *should* is a red flag that an unhelpful thought is in progress!)

Here was her first attempt at crafting a statement:

Try 1 → *I enjoy working out 5 times a week.* (Seriously? Do you REALLY? Client: No, but I feel like I "should" enjoy it.) Let's make it more authentic and believable.
Here was her second attempt:
Try 2 → *I exercise so I can move easier and be pain-free.* (Closer, but still, a little work to do.) I suggested that she craft the statement so that she could easily perform the action, and it's easy to believe the result.
Try 3 → *I experience joy when I move my body daily in fun, lighthearted ways through dance and walking.* (Yes! The client can easily feel herself experiencing joy while she walks and dances! Bingo!)

Each time, I had the client check in and see what part of the statement felt truthful and what part felt false. We were looking for a believable statement that stretched her and invited her into action, affirming her success instead of beating her up for not acting.

Now every time she reads that statement, she partners it with a clear image of how much she enjoys dance and walking. It calls her to enjoy the present moment and rewires the negative "should" in her brain. She can also take immediate action on it. Every time she moves her body in a fun light-hearted way, it reinforces the truth of her new confidence-building statement, giving her a little success each day.

Once she is comfortable with this statement and living it out, she can adjust it to stretch herself to a new level. The revision might look like this: I love the toned body I create through 30 minutes of daily dance. I love my body and myself enough to give it consistent joyful exercise.

New Perspective = New Results

Confidence-building statements invite us to visualize a new result in our minds, acting as a new map or GPS-like destination for the brain. Once the brain can form a picture of the desired outcome, it is believable and the results come quicker.

Powerful confidence-building statements that include believability and effective action rewire the brain for change and create the following chain reaction:

- Rewires the automatic response of the brain.
- New thought is generated.
- Changed thoughts lead to new choices.
- New choices create new outcomes!
- New outcomes increase self-confidence.

Here are some ideas on how to implement these statements into your daily life. I've used each of these practices myself!

- Select 10 statements to begin your practice. Write them in your journal every day.
- Get a pack of recipe cards and write one confidence-building statement per card. Carry them with you and review them several times a day. Create a practice of reviewing them when you get up and go to bed. Right after you wake up and before you go to bed are optimal times for new ideas to sink deeper into your subconscious.
- Record your confidence-building statements in an audio format and listen to them. Most cell phones have a voice recorder, so it's quick and easy to do this! Then make a practice of listening to your recording several times a day!
- Create a 3-5-minute mind movie with images representing the outcome and the statements and watch it daily.
- Set a reminder on your phone with the statements. Set it to go off hourly when you are first using a new statement. Then back it off to 1x a day and then 1x per week as you feel like this statement becomes your new dominant way of thinking.

Stories of Confidence-Building Statements

Kim became my client while in the process of leaving a long-term relationship that had turned out less than fulfilling for her. In fact, she left feeling full of doubt, not certain if there was anything better for her, and confused by the toxic messages from her former partner. One of the first things we began to work on was the negative conversations she was having with herself in her head. It was a great opportunity to begin working on confidence-building statements. Here's how she describes it in her own words:

> *"I was a person who did a lot of negative thinking and looping. If I had a conversation and I didn't like the way it went, I would fester on it and it would eat away at me, thinking about it constantly and even not sleeping. I was stuck in these thoughts all of the time and couldn't escape them. When I met Vicki one of the first things she said was to write down 10 confidence-building statements a day - so for a year and a half, I wrote 10-14 statements every day. This helped me to break the negative thinking cycles. I had to do this as a precursor to stepping into more confident living. I was so determined to break the cycle of negative thinking. I consistently wrote my statements and if I missed one day I wrote them double the next day."*
>
> *— Kim, Wyoming, teacher*

Kim successfully broke her negative thinking habit! Today she has gone on to pursue a career more aligned with her gifts. She is moving to an area of the country that feels like a better fit for her soul and is about to sign the closing papers on her brand-new house!

Kicking the negative thinking loop by using confidence-building statements opened an entirely new world of possibilities for Kim!

Confidence-building statements literally changed my life. Nothing I have done or accomplished today could have happened had it not been for the life-changing shift these statements created in me. Just like Kim, I also had a habit of focusing on the negative. Once I learned the life-changing power of these statements, I created an affirmative statement for every thought I noticed that did not support my health and well-being. Money, career, parenting, body image… my deck of cards grew and grew. I used recipe cards, wrote each statement down on a card, and then reviewed it as many times a day as I could. After just a short time of using them, I noticed changes in my thinking. Motivated by that success, I continued. I carried my deck of cards with me everywhere I went, and they became a lifeline pulling me thought by thought out of a deep murky sea. As one statement felt completely assimilated into my new way of thinking and being, I retired the card. Today I keep those old cards as a reminder of where I began and how far I have journeyed.

Now that you have learned how to create confidence-building statements and how to use them to shift your own thoughts, I want to remind you of the power this one small practice has to shift the trajectory of your life completely. It's like upgrading the operating system on your computer. Your new "upgraded" operating system empowers you to make new choices in your life that would not have been possible before. These statements re-write the neural pathways in your brain: what once seemed impossible now becomes possible.

Commit to regular practice for as long as it takes. You may have wanted me to say "practice the statements for 7 days or 21 days" - the typical advice we get on creating a habit. That's not what I'm here to tell you. Commit to the daily practice of the statements until they become as true for you as it is to look at the color blue and say, "that's blue." When you have internalized your statements as complete truth, then it's time to re-write them and stretch yourself to a new level.

This one practice has the power to change your life in amazing ways. Now let's add on the next powerful practice!

CHAPTER 3 - CREATING CONSISTENT CONNECTION

"The quieter you become the more you are able to hear."
— *Rumi*

Key Practice 2 - Listening to Heart-Centered Intuitive Guidance

What does it mean to connect with heart-centered intuition? In this chapter, we are going to explore what it looks like to be in constant connection with your inner guide - the highest, most resourceful part of yourself. There have been many names given to this: intuition, source, spirit, gut feeling, and inner guide. It's that wise, steadfast spirit in you that is not restricted by the human form. This wise guiding inner spirit gets disconnected by layers of conditioning. The conditioning disconnects you from your authentic self and causes you to feel lost, confused, and alone.

To understand this more completely, let's look at the different components of consciousness:

Our consciousness can be thought of in three parts: the subconscious mind, the conscious mind, and the higher consciousness. The Subconscious (sometimes referred to as the unconscious mind; for our purposes here, we will use the terms interchangeably) is always recording everything that happens in our world and storing it for future reference. The subconscious has recorded every memory, interaction, and learning moment, and then filtered it according to what it views as important. The subconscious processes innumerable bits of information at a time.

Our conscious mind is the analytical part we use daily for thinking, driving, and speaking. It can process about 5-7 bits of information at a time, so it has a limited capacity to what it can process at any given moment. Our conscious mind partners with the subconscious to recall important facts, memories, and knowledge. We don't need to hold all of that in our conscious minds.

The Higher Consciousness speaks through our heart-centered intuition. It's the part of you that is unchanging (it's the lifeforce in a baby that's the same as the lifeforce on a deathbed), and it is connected to the greater power of the universe. This connection transcends religion and faith and is unique to each of us. Your Higher Consciousness is always guiding you on the path toward your greatest potential, and that has been its job since you showed up as a tiny bundle of possibilities. This connection is pure love, and we learn to listen to it by connecting with our heart and intuitive inner guidance.

The problem is that most people operate from their conscious mind and only occasionally tap into the ever-present heart-centered wisdom. Learning to partner listening to the clear quiet voice of heart-centered intuition changes our entire perspective.

On the occasion that an individual experiences their heart-centered voice, they may say I had a "gut" feeling or "I just knew with all my heart that this is what I had to do." But most people do not know how to access that intuition for daily use and guidance. So, they end up living from the conscious mind space, which functions from fear rather than love. The mind space is full of doubt, it second-guesses, and at its best, it drives you crazy with thoughts that feel like they spin and chase each other - sometimes referred to as "Monkey Mind!"

Tapping into the heart-centered intuition is a totally new way of showing up to life, which leads to living from a deeper, more connected place than your spinning monkey mind. Living by intuition will lead you to new ever-increasing levels of joy. It invites a new way of living by leading with your intuitive heart rather than with the ego mind.

What Does it Replace?

Living from a place of heart-centered intuitive guidance replaces operating only from the conscious mind or ego. Here are some signs that the ego mind is in control:
- Over relying on the advice and opinions of others as your basis for decision making.
- Desiring to be certain of an outcome before acting.
- Relying only on facts, statistics, data for decision making.
- Perfectionism. I can't do XYZ until I know it will be "right."
- Confusion. Constantly saying "I don't know," or feeling lost.
- Old stories come up explaining why you can't do things. These stories are based on past "failures" and conditioned messages you have received from others.
- You have "monkey mind." Swirling, rapid thoughts that make it seem impossible to decide anything.

Earlier in Chapter one, we discussed the five most common experiences that condition or separate us from who we really are. Each one of those experiences acts as a layer of distortion between you and your heart. You need to begin identifying those layers of conditioned experiences and beliefs. Understanding you are not your conditioning unlocks the voice of your inner wisdom.

You begin to experience life in new ways with each layer that peels away as clarity and connection re-emerge. Here are some ways you can expect your life to change:
- You may seek expert knowledge as information for decision making, yet you completely trust yourself to discern how that information applies to you and make the best decision for yourself.
- You learn to trust that heart-led decisions often don't make

rational sense and that you can trust the outcome no matter what it is, as your heart is ALWAYS leading you on the path of your greatest potential.
- Heart-centered intuitive answers are always very clear and certain. The entire path may not be clear, but the NEXT step is always clear, and when it isn't, you can patiently wait for clarity, knowing it will arrive with optimal timing.
- There is no such thing as "perfect." Perfect is a standard created by the mind and a cumulative collection of other people's values and preferences. Instead, we begin seeing outcomes as "feed-forward information" information that helps us make the next optimal choice.
- Heart-centered awareness sees old stories and recognizes them for what they are. It doesn't need to reject them, make them bad, or chase them away -- it just sees and chooses to refocus its awareness on the still small intuitive voice, learning to trust it completely.
- Instead of getting involved in the monkey mind and feeling like you are twirling around the hamster wheel, heart-centered intuition awareness allows you to step back, watch the activity of the mind and extend compassion instead of judgment.

Therefore, learning to connect to your heart-centered intuition becomes the single most important skill to help you live daily in complete confidence. Trusting the intuitive voice of your soul is the strongest most accurate guiding compass you can have.

Daily Practice - How to Connect to Heart-Centered Intuition

Two significant practices return you to a complete connection with your soul: mindfulness and inner voice journaling. Using these two practices alone is transformational— partnering them with all five key confidence-building practices accelerates growth and change. These practices quiet the mind enough so that you can hear the voice of your soul speak.

Mindfulness

Our mind is the primary distractor from listening to our inner guidance. It shouts, bullies, and repeats what Grandma told you years ago, and creates stories out of mere hints and suggestions. This frenetic spinning of the monkey mind causes anxiety, doubt, fear, and regret. It causes you to second-guess, even when you sense you are on the right path.

The egoic mind causes anxiety by dwelling in one of two places: the past or the future, neither of which you can do anything about in the present moment. Mindfulness is the practice of giving your attention solely to the present moment, to whatever is in front of you.

Here is a chart that will help you understand the difference between the mind and heart-centered intuition:

Characteristics of the Mind	Characteristics of the Inner Voice
Loud & demanding	Quiet, soft, bubbling up
Doubtful & looping over the same things	Certain, clear, confident
Harsh, critical, judgmental	Peaceful
Reminds you of criticism from others	Feels aligned
Doesn't trust	Trusts
Anxious, worried, regretting	Always in the present moment

Mindfulness techniques help you shift from the monkey mind to the clarity and peace of your authentic inner self. Here are some forms of mindfulness you could consider practicing:
- Meditation is a form of mindfulness that essentially is the intentional practice of being present.
- Take a daily walk and focus your attention on nature.
- Take 15 minutes in the morning to drink your cup of coffee with no distractions.
- Pause for 5-15 minutes to focus on sounds, colors, textures, and smells around you.
- Body awareness scan - what is your body feeling at this moment?

Mindfulness is also about slowing down long enough to create space to listen to your inner voice. Too often in our busy culture, we compete for the busyness trophy. It can feel easier to be constantly in motion than to spend a few moments by ourselves.

Years ago, I felt my life spinning at 90 miles an hour from the moment I got up until the moment I dropped into bed. I knew this wasn't helpful or productive, especially given the clarity I was seeking about life (see the next Key Practice!). Change is easier when practiced in small chunks, so I decided to take 15 minutes every morning to drink my coffee before I started the day. No more slamming my coffee in a to-go mug and rocketing out the door.

This simple change made my days flow easier, and I noticed that the days were more chaotic when I missed my 15 minutes. This 15-minute commitment eventually led to a much more mindful way of living throughout the entire day.

One of my favorite teachers on mindfulness is Eckhart Tolle, particularly his book *The Power of Now*. This is a great resource for additional learning on this subject.

Inner Voice Journaling

Journaling is another key daily practice that helps you learn to recognize and listen to your own true, authentic inner voice. I call this a practice because it requires a regular commitment to strengthening your intuitive muscle and to developing the trust of what and who you are hearing along the way. It might be frustrating at first. In fact, it's common at first that we "try so hard" to hear the inner voice that we miss it. Relax. When you hear the voice, you will know it. Refer to the chart above for the characteristics of the inner voice. It takes time to cultivate a relationship with it, so it feels safe to come out and speak. Treat this as getting to know someone you have never met before that you desire to know intimately.

The best way I have found to do this is through the practice of inner voice journaling. Let's take a look at the practice:

You write - the heart listens
You listen - the heart writes

It's a good idea to get a journal specifically for this practice. While you are at it, grab a few colored pens too! Decide on a time of day when you can make this a regular practice. It's a great idea to start by writing the 10 confidence-building statements you chose in the exercise above!

Once you are ready to begin inner-voice writing, start with an opening statement like: *"Please speak to me clearly and show me what I need to be, know, and do today. I invite help from all angels, guides, and those that support my greatest and highest good."*

Then begin by writing a question you would like the answer to. I'll give you some starting questions for practice so you can begin to discern the voice that is your inner guide more clearly. It's tempting to dive right into the big questions you want answers to but allow yourself some relationship-building time to work up to that.

Select the color of ink "you" will write in and begin your journal question with an arrow (→). As you become proficient at this journaling technique, it's fun to reflect back on the learning and insights you received. Getting in the habit of using the → for your voice shows where you were speaking or listening.

Once you have journaled your question, switch ink colors and open your inner voice writing line with ∞. The infinity symbol (∞) is a great reminder of how the inner voice writing process happens. You ask a question, the voice responds, and you respond to the voice and listen again for its answer. It becomes a never-ending loop of communication straight from your inner being!

Once you open with ∞ and listen, write word-for-word what bubbles up from your heart.

Here's how to know what voice you're listening for. The ego analytical voice of the head is noisy, talks fast, criticizes, doubts, is uncertain, and changes its opinion frequently. You know that voice too well already, and it's not the one you are listening for here! The intuitive inner voice is calm and confident, speaks slower sometimes in short phrases at first, and is always loving and kind. It doesn't always make logical sense! (Refer to the chart above for a full range of characteristics of both voices.)

Here are some questions to use to begin your intuitive journaling practice:

→ What am I 100% certain of?

∞

→ Who loves me unconditionally?

∞

→ What is the greatest gift I have to give others?

∞

→ What's the greatest gift I can give myself?

∞

Once you tap into the flow of your intuitive voice, practice tuning into it on a regular basis. You will begin to recognize it as the amazing guide and friend it is. Then you begin the journey of learning to trust what the voice speaks and enter a new ever-deepening trust of who you are.

Nothing erases self-doubt quicker than complete trust in yourself, who you are, and what you are. Your intuitive, inner voice will connect you straight back to that pure, amazing, brilliant person you have always been.

New Perspective = New Results

The consistent feelings of self-doubt, second-guessing, and the need to seek approval from others release as your trust in yourself deepens and self-confidence blooms. The change this creates in your daily life will quickly be noticeable to yourself and others. Think about the areas where you have self-doubt. Your job? Parenting? Dealing with a difficult ex-partner? Managing difficult employees? When you partner with your inner guiding voice to confidently deal with these situations, you will find yourself experiencing a renewed energy for life. No longer is your energy being drained away by self-doubt and worry. Instead, confidence fosters energy and life. You will find situations, people, and perspectives that once clouded your every thought begin to disappear out of your world. In their place will be new, more aligned friends, opportunities, and ideas. Joy, peace, confidence, and purpose become your new best friends.

Listen to the story of how Heather was guided away from her soul-sucking career toward her dream home!

Stories of Connection

Ever since puberty, I began to second-guess myself. I stopped listening to that voice which was pretty clear and strong prior to that. I've led a life that doesn't fully feel like me and feels like an unfinished story. During our annual gathering of friends, a mutual friend recommended that I consider coaching with Vicki. From the get-go, Vicki had an amazing ability to get to the heart of things quickly. She helped me focus and get there fast.

The tools and techniques she offered helped me to realize that the voice and the answers I was seeking were inside of me all along! It's been powerful stuff - I'm 57 and have had a few false starts where I started to get on track and then doubted myself and fell back off again. Now I understand life is short! I get it in a visceral way. The wise insightful guidance I received through Vicki's coaching and my desire for more meaning in my life has combined into this perfect circumstance that has inspired me to dig deeper.

Coaching helped me listen to what I had known all along-- it's time to leave the job that has brought me no satisfaction. At the same time, I was considering my career future, my dream home came on the market. It didn't seem to make logical sense to purchase it and none of my friends or family thought it was a good idea. It was located in a rural part of California that I had very little connection to, yet my intuition was clearly guiding me to do it! It felt so aligned! It was a radical act, but this process of connecting back to my true self gave me the courage to act.

Two months in, this home is my absolutely incredible happy place where I can go, feel genuinely lucky, and begin to reimagine something different. Everyone thought I was crazy, but I did it anyway, and it is already serving me in such big ways.

I realized I had to stop listening to the outside world and what people are telling me, even the people I know and love. Instead, I've learned to turn inward and listen for and follow what my gut says to do. Now I know the clarity of that much stronger voice inside of me. It feels clear and so remarkably solid. When anxiety and fear arise, which of course they still do, I can turn to my practices of meditation, walking, being present, and journaling. They've given me some distance between me and my strong emotions, and I've learned to let the emotional waves of fear and anxiety simply flow over me and pass. I start every morning with a short meditation and a walk, and these practices really help keep me grounded every day. I remain curious and witness my emotions without getting nearly as attached to them. These practices clear the deck enough so that I can hear my intuition more clearly.

Learning to trust and connect to my inner guidance gave me my life back on my own terms. I have my mojo back! I don't know exactly where this is all leading, but I trust in the process, and I have not felt this aligned in decades! It's so liberating to cast off the regret about the fear and self-doubt that kept me playing small for so long.

I have rediscovered the creative, lighter, more courageous, loving, and empowered woman that has always lived inside of me and that is so joyful! I feel insanely lucky, and very grateful to Vicki for her wise guidance, and to the rather magical and awe-inspiring universe which is starting to act like it has my back.

— Heather, California, realtor

In 2018 I was ending a visit with my dear friend Janet. It was our last meal together after spending a beautiful week hiking and enjoying each other's company. As we wrapped up our final goodbye, Janet said she wanted to propose an experiment or challenge. She proposed that we commit to making decisions by listening only to our intuitive inner voice and doing what it said, even when it didn't make sense, for 90 days. I immediately agreed—with the caveat that if I was going to commit, it needed to be a year-long commitment.

That challenge led to a year of decisions that paved the way for me to leave my corporate job almost exactly one year later, in May of 2019. I knew that was the direction I was moving in, yet I never was "quite" ready. Listening to my inner voice gently guided and pushed me forward and helped me find the courage and confidence to do what I needed. This experiment changed my life completely and forever. It taught me gently, step by step, how to trust myself—my true authentic self—and it guided me to make decisions that brought me closer into alignment with the authentic me. I still faced a lot of emotions along the way, but, knowing without a shadow of a doubt, that I was being guided by my intuition kept me confidently moving forward. The toughest day was the day I handed in my resignation letter. It seemed like such a finality. No turning back. As I sat with my nervous stomach, waiting for my boss that day, I heard my inner spirit quietly say, "It's just the next step. It's no more or less significant than any of the other courageous steps, it's just the next one." This quieted my spirit, and almost three years later, I have never regretted handing my boss that resignation.

CHAPTER 4 - BE GUIDED BY A CLEAR VISION OF THE FUTURE

"Your visions will become clear only when you can look into your own heart. Who looks outside, dreams; he who looks inside, awakens."
— Carl Jung

Key Practice 3 - Clarity

Confidence-building statements rewire the brain. Connection is a direct path back to powerful inner wisdom and knowing. Clarity acts as the guiding beacon that pulls us forward to a new reality.

It's quite common for a client to begin coaching with me by sharing a greater vision of what they want in their life and simultaneously feel confused about why they have this vision and feel stuck and unable to reach it. Let me describe it to you like this:

Pretend you are standing on the bank of the most beautiful river. Across the river, on the other shore, you can see some images that beckon you strongly, but the early morning mist rising from the water distorts the images making it hard to see them clearly. With all your heart, you want to jump right into that river and swim across to be in this other world that you suspect would perfectly complement your soul. You look at the water, full of mud and dirt, even some greenish slime. Someone also told you there might be alligators and even biting fish in the river. On top of that, because it's so muddy, you cannot see the bottom or how deep it is. If you knew you could cross safely, you most certainly would, but with all these dangers lurking, it's far safer to stay put. No matter how much you try to convince yourself to stay, however, that vision of what's on the other side calls to you like a siren in the ocean. You can't ignore it or get it out of your mind.

Clarity is about being certain of what's beckoning you from the other side. By "certain," I don't mean knowing the exact description and outcome of it.

Four years ago, the hazy shapes on the other side of my "river" beckoned to me:
- I wanted work that more fully aligned with my zone of strength
- I wanted a workplace that valued my contribution
- I desired flexibility and freedom to travel and work from wherever I was
- I wanted to live in a warmer climate

These ideas and images kept beating inside me no matter how much I tried to ignore them. I had many questions and doubts about how I would reach the other side of my "river." I needed clarity-- not of the specifics of what was on the other side-- but of the very next step for me to take. However, that meant knowing the approximate direction I was headed in: a new career, a traveling lifestyle, and someday warmer weather!

Often, we have that sense of hazy, deeper life purpose and calling, and yet, life is so busy that we never pause to understand the inner urge. Connection comes before clarity. Learning to be mindful and connecting to your inner guiding voice facilitates the "dirt settling" out of the water so clarity can emerge. It's crucial to know that when you have a lack of clarity, it's a sign to strengthen the connection to your inner voice. Once you have the connection, clarity emerges naturally, the larger picture comes into focus, and the very next steps become obvious.

It is important to note, that healing trauma is a necessary step on the path to complete freedom and clarity. If you continually feel stuck on any step, it could be a sign that healing work is needed. This work is best done with a trauma-trained coach, therapist, or counselor.

As clarity emerges through mindfulness and connection, it will serve you well to ask yourself key exploratory questions about what you truly desire in life. A recent client came to me and shared that one of her top priorities in life was finding a life partner. She was frustrated that it wasn't happening. Very quickly, I learned that she had no clear idea of what she wanted that partnership to look like, and therefore she could not have specific steps on how to connect with a partner.

I'm not talking about the type of egoic law of attraction principles where you list the physical characteristics of your ideal partner and the balance of their bank account. That's only minimally helpful in finding a life partner. Instead, my client needed to be clear on what her ideal partnership looked like. She quickly got into this and identified that she wanted a partner who shared interests with her but also had his own interests, someone that could carry on an intelligent, witty conversation, and a partner that had quality relationships with friends and family.

Most people spend more time planning their ideal vacation than understanding what their ideal, thriving life would look like. It's important that you spend some time considering what a thriving life would look like for you. Clarity comes first in your mind. In my client's case, once she identified the high-level qualities she wanted in a partner, it gave her clear action steps to finding that partner. First and foremost, was she exemplifying the qualities that she wanted in her partner? If not, then attracting what she wanted would be difficult.

I believe we are each born with knowing inside us that shows up in the form of desire and inner longing. It's unique for everyone. Those deep desires and inner longings are clues to what optimal life would, or could, look like.

If you feel completely lost or clueless as to what your ideal life would look like, don't panic! You are not alone. This is just a sign that conditioning has disconnected you from your authentic self, and it's time to get reconnected!

Trauma, cultural conditioning, limiting beliefs, family patterns, and religion are all layers of distortion covering up your true self. These deep forms of conditioning keep us from owning the true desires of our hearts. I believe the quiet desires of your heart are from the still small voice inside of you asking you to return to prioritizing what's best for you.

For many years, I suffered living in a climate that had extremely cold winters. I constantly desired to live in a warmer climate, but I allowed my job, family, and obligations to keep me living and shivering through the winters. Then I got serious about what would be optimal for me in all areas of my life. I began spending chunks of time in a warmer climate during the winter whenever I could. It became clear that for me to thrive, I needed to get serious about aligning with what was best for my body and health. I dreamed about this and then held it as a firm intention. Then I acted to discover a new career I could do remotely. I also made the most of every moment of the last few years of raising my children while I waited for the time to move south.

As I write this segment of the book, I am sitting on the rooftop of my apartment in Mazatlán, Mexico. It's reality—I'm working, living, and loving my warmer climate. But it all started with me getting a clear picture of where I was headed. I didn't have all the details, and I didn't know "how" I would make it happen. The "how" is not even important at this point. Clarity of direction is what guides us toward what we desire.

What is Clarity?

Clarity is the clear knowing and understanding of what a thriving life looks like for you. For some, it's a clearly defined purpose or life mission. For others, it is made apparent by living a life filled with the opposite of what they desire. A soul-sucking job that drives you crazy is a good indicator that you would love work that energizes you and aligns more closely with your gifts and skillset. Difficult relationships (whether romantic, at work, or with friends) are an indicator that your heart desires thriving relationships. You seek people who are mutually respectful, supportive, and value genuine partnerships in which everyone takes responsibility for themselves. The more connected you become (Key Practice 2) the more clarity you will have.

Clarity acts like programming your GPS to receive directions. Before Google Maps can give you a recommended route to your destination, you have to tell it where you desire to go. It's the same on a universal level. You have to be clear on the destination you want to go and then let the universe show you the map of how to get there. Don't forget to be flexible and invite the universe to take you to an even better destination than planned! You can borrow my motto "This or something better, please!"

I believe that we each chose to be born with a clear purpose and mission, yet human life and conditioning causes us to forget that choice until we intentionally begin reconnecting with it.

What doe Clarity Replace?

Clarity most simply replaces confusion and doubt. Where confusion exists, no forward progress can be made. Confusion keeps us "safe" and in our "comfort zone," and it causes us to settle for less than what we deserve and are capable of receiving and achieving. Confusion becomes an opportunity to acknowledge the circumstances, shortcomings, and problems that we don't currently have the skill set to solve-- and then pushes us to develop the skills to find new solutions. Any life challenge that presents itself can be tackled and moved through with the best toolbox of skills.

Where does the unexpected fit in? Sometimes a tragic accident occurs, or you receive a difficult diagnosis. All of our careful planning is wiped out in the time it takes to answer the unexpected phone call. We can choose to look at these as universally guided detours that are always supporting us even when we don't understand on a logical level. My greatest gifts of learning and growth came from experiences I would never have consciously chosen for myself. When these moments come surrender to a higher plan that you can't see and ride the wave until clarity comes.

Creating a New Map of Reality

If your current reality has you up at night, regretting the past or worrying about the future, then it's time to begin using your imagination to build a new map for yourself. Our brain is just like a computer. It doesn't recognize the difference between reality and imagination. So, in this practice, I will teach you how to tap into your imagination to create a new map of your future.

I call this pulling yourself forward to your future! It is much more enjoyable than being a pawn of your past. Think of this as learning a new skill: if you have not used your imagination much, it's a little rusty. If you were told as a child to get your head out of the clouds and back to reality, then I'm giving you permission to stick your head back into the clouds!

Let's get started with the act of dreaming. In the how-to section, you will find a series of journal questions and a life wheel to assist you in this new practice.

For now, I want you to begin to visualize your life as if it were a wheel.

Each section of spokes represents a section of your life. The most common sections people use are:
- Career
- Finances
- Health
- Relationships
- Spirituality
- Recreation
- Contribution

Some may add other categories like dating relationships, ideal geographical location, educational goals, skills they would like to acquire, or bucket-filling activities.

Consider each category using the following scale:
   0 = completely unsatisfied
   10 = the best that you can imagine

How would you rate each category today? Maybe you are unhappy with your career, so it gets a 3, but you are very happy with your relationships, and that category gets a 7. When you have ranked each area consider how "balanced" your life wheel is. Are all the categories fairly aligned, or did it become quickly evident why life feels a bit out of balance for you?

The next part is where the fun begins. For this piece, you really have to let go of one question: How? This is not the time to assess if something is possible or probable or how it would be accomplished. This is the time to allow your imagination to soar and begin to ask:

If I was Living a Level 10 Thriving Life in Every Area, What Would That Look Like?

Here is a list of questions to consider for each of the common life areas:

CAREER
- If I was living a level 10 in my career, what would I be doing?
- What wouldn't I be doing?
- Who would I be doing it with?
- How would I be doing it?
- How much would I be earning doing it?
- What types of relationships would I want to have with my coworkers?
- How do we all get along?
- Do I work at a physical location? Remote?

FINANCES
- What causes me stress financially?
- What would I be able to do, say or be if all my needs were abundantly met?
- Who is a resource to mentor me financially?
- How could I grow financially if I let go of my limiting money beliefs?

HEALTH
- What is going well with my health?
- What could be better about my health?
- What would it feel like to be in optimal health? (Make sure to not get caught in cultural conditioning of measuring health success by body size and numbers on a scale)
- How would my health and wellbeing change if I let go of feeling responsible for others?
- What climate serves my greatest health and wellbeing?

RELATIONSHIPS
- What would my ideal romantic partnership look like (if you are in a relationship or not)
- What is serving me now in relationships and what is not?
- What would my relationships look like if they fully supported me in every aspect?
- How would I ideally interact with my kids, parents, in-laws?
- What would it be like if all my relationships were respectful, everyone took responsibility for themselves, and each individual owned their gifts and talents?
- What would it feel like to let go of having to "do it all?"

SPIRITUALITY
- How would it feel to be clearly connected to my own spirit?
- What would you do, be or say if you fully trusted your connection with the universe and your inner guidance?
- What would it feel like to honor everything your spirit is saying every day?
- How would it feel to own that you are worthy and deserving of anything and everything?
- What would it feel like if you finally trusted that you ARE enough?

RECREATION
- What would life feel like if you had an ideal balance of work and recreation?
- What new skills or hobbies would you learn?
- Who would you enjoy recreation with?
- What if you viewed recreation and recharging your battery as a necessity rather than an option?

What other area of life that is unique to you do you need to consider as a category? This is the time to explore what level 10 living looks like in EVERY area of your life.

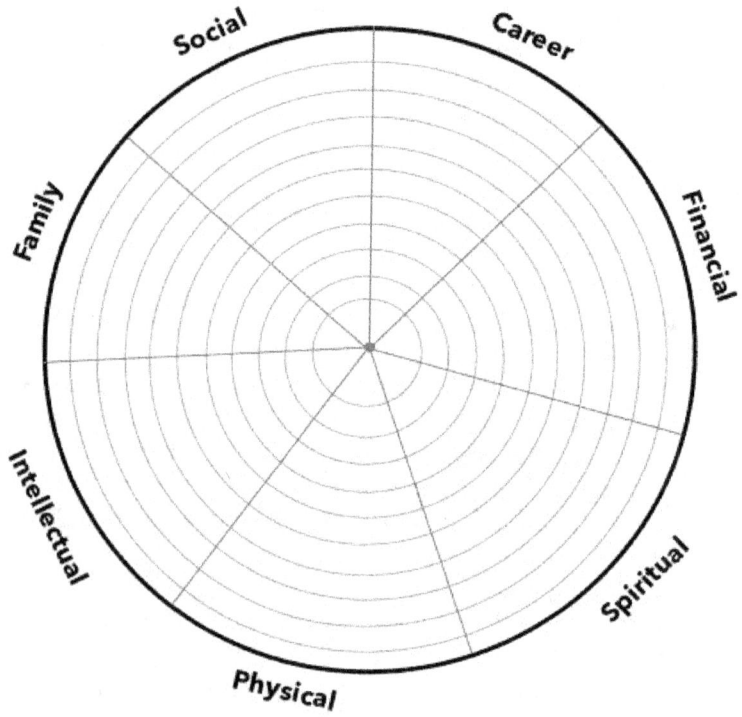

Download a complete guided exercise at www.vickihaddock.com.

Daily Practice - How to Visualize your Life at Level 10

Now that you have spent some time designing your Level 10 Life, it's time to begin embracing this dream on a daily basis!

Practice spending 5 minutes each day imagining your Level 10 Life. Imagine it as if it was already here. What does it feel like to be living this best life? Then ask yourself: what is one action step I could take today to move me in the direction of my best life? Then take that action step.

Overwhelm warning At this stage most of my clients spend a moment in panic thinking, "There is no way I can make this happen." They then begin to list all of the obstacles and reasons why it's not possible.

Overwhelming emotions happen when one looks at a goal and sees all of the things that would need to change in order to get to the goal. You don't NEED to see all the steps along the path. It's not even humanly possible to do all the steps at once. All you need to do is program your "destination" in your mental GPS and then learn to act on the one thing in front of you in the present moment.

It's no different from physically needing to drive your car each mile of a 1,000-mile journey. There are lots of unknowns along the way and lots of choices. Will you get a flat tire along the way? Will you take the scenic route or the interstates? Will you stop for a week to visit friends or drive straight through? In what town will you need to stop for gas?

None of this actually matters as long as you are headed in the direction of your best life and focusing on enjoying each step of the journey. We can only show up in THIS very moment.

Let me share another secret with you: it's not actually about the destination even. This exercise is really not about helping you arrive at level 10 in all areas...but please don't throw the book down now! It's about teaching you the skills to step by step, moment by moment, to act towards your best life. Destinations shift and change. When you reach your "Level 8" relationships you will have a new perspective on what Level 10 relationships look like and your destination will shift - and that's 100% OK the important part is that you are on the journey. Enjoy the daily steps.

You have to live each moment anyway, so why not live them taking steps to create your best life!

New Perspective = New Results

This skill of finding clarity affords you the ability to become unstuck very quickly. No matter how bad or good your situation or what action you can or can't take today, you can ALWAYS take 5 minutes to imagine and feel your best life. Our minds are good at allowing the fears, doubts, and worst outcomes to dance and play. You get to choose what you give your attention to - and what you give your attention to grows!

Momentum and excitement come naturally when you see small and then large changes unfolding in your life. It naturally reinforces new neural pathways of success!

Stories of Finding Clarity

Brian, an executive leader from Virginia, came to me through my executive coaching practice. Our conversations began in the middle of some corporate shuffles at the company he worked for. What once had been a great environment and team to work with had shifted and was still shifting in uncertain ways. Brian was feeling off-balance and confused about whether to continue investing time and energy in his current position or whether to begin hunting for a different opportunity that matched his deep skill set.

Throughout our coaching conversations, Brian claimed his new confidence-building statement: "I own my own destiny." Next, he turned an eye inwards and began to reconnect with his authentic self. He discovered his core values of connection, influence, adventure, and impact.

He gained a clear understanding of why his current role - as it had now evolved - felt so frustrating to him. His need for one-on-one connection and to provide value to others based on his deep wisdom and skillset were missing, having been reduced as the organization reshuffled. He also understood that the impact of two years of reducing travel and in-person connections due to the Covid 19 pandemic had taken its toll. Adventure and in-person connection are two key things that give Brian energy and recharge his battery. He used these key insights to shift into Key Practice 3 - Clarity - and that is where the magic happened!

Through coaching, he gave himself permission to own his own value, and worth, and to look at what a Level 10 living would look like for himself, his career, and his family. Brian walked away from coaching with a 3-legged approach to creating his optimal career path that completely honors his skillset, his love of adventure, and his desire to make an impact.

This plan also gives him complete clarity on what the next step of action is in each area of his 3-legged approach to creating his Level 10 Life.

Living life without clarity is like being blindfolded, spun in circles, and then asked to hit the target's bullseye with the dart you have in your hand. It's not likely to happen! Clarity gives one the ability to aim directly for the bullseye.

Eight years ago, I learned how to use this clarity technique. It has changed every aspect of my life significantly and completely shifted me in a new direction. When I did this exercise for the first time, I began to dream about finding a way to travel more and work while I was traveling. At the time this Level 10 Life was developing, I had a child who was a senior in high school and one that was a freshman. From a "be realistic" standpoint there were a lot of years and obstacles in between me making this life a reality! My job was very hands-on, and I had 2 kids in school still! But that did not stop me from using my imagination and becoming clear about what I wanted. Here are some things I got very clear on:

- I needed to develop a new career that allowed me to work remotely
- I wanted work that allowed me to focus more time in my zone of strength
- The cold climate I lived in was not conducive to my greatest health.
- I was going to be completely present and supportive for every bit of my kids' school experience
- I loved to travel and adventure and wanted more of it even if I could not make that my lifestyle 100% yet.

Defining my Level 10 Life gave me clarity on what next steps I needed to take on the path. Here's what that looked like:

⇒ I took steps to search out a new career that I could do remotely and that matched my skillset (that's how I found professional coaching!)
⇒ Once I found that career, I took the steps to get the training, education, and experience needed to position myself for success as a coach.
⇒ I financially planned my exit from my corporate job. I paid down my debt and planned my financial transition.
⇒ I began traveling 2-3 weeks of the year to warmer climates.
⇒ I took steps to find ways to make myself more comfortable in the cold climate I lived in until I had the opportunity to leave the cold weather.
⇒ I was fully engaged in every aspect of my kids' final years of high school, ending their experience well!

Today I'm embracing my life in Mexico, enjoying a flexible remote work lifestyle in a climate that I thrive in. I'm enjoying continued connection with my family (although it looks a bit different today!), and my location and connections.

The Journey: It wasn't always clear to me that I would arrive where I am today; in fact, now that I have arrived, there are new goals and dreams I'm moving towards. Along the journey, I became a better version of myself. Each step forward released another layer of doubt and cemented a new layer of confidence. I understand today that my desires and goals have been the vehicle that the universe has used for continued personal growth, enlightenment, and joy. Even though I love living in a warmer climate, if the universe moves me back to a cold climate I will experience the same joy, love, and synchronicity as I do in Mexico-- my happiness does not depend on an outcome or external circumstance. It is always inside of me. Where I go, there I always am. I'm no longer seeking because I have found myself.

Today I am absolutely the most confident version of myself to date! I'm excited to continue my growth journey and embrace ever-increasing levels of joy, abundance, happiness, and confidence!

You may have heard the ancient quote, "Where there is no vision the people perish." Wise King Solomon penned that in the book of Proverbs. When there is no vision, feelings of overwhelm, depression, and stuck ness can take over. When one embraces the beautiful gifts of dreaming and imagination and honors the deep desires of one's own heart, clarity and vision come quickly. The details fill in as needed!

I'm giving you permission to dream! To own what you really want! You are worthy and deserving of having the desires of your heart. When you follow these five key practices in order, once you have your daily confidence-building statement practice in progress, and you begin connecting to your heart on a regular basis -- then clarity is a natural next step!

It's life-changing! Program that life-GPS and then trust that each step is taking you in the optimal path towards your destination! Even when detours happen - which they will - c to hold the clarity and vision of your destination, allowing flexibility on how you will arrive there!

CHAPTER 5 - CONFIDENT COMMUNICATION
LEARN TO SAY ANYTHING TO ANYONE WHILE BEING RESPECTFUL TO EVERYONE

"Communication is like riding a bicycle or typing. If you are willing to work at it you can rapidly improve the quality of every part of your life."
— *Brian Tracy*

"If you just communicate you can get by. But if you communicate skillfully you can work miracles."
— *Jim Rohn*

Key Practice 4 – Developing the Skill of Confident Communication

You are well on your way to creating a new life just by using the previous 3 confidence-building keys already presented here. I'm betting if you have been applying as you read, you have already noticed some changes! Our 4th key is the key that unlocks massive change in relation to how you interact with others. The three previous keys could be viewed as predominantly internal changes, while this key will begin to shift interactions for you externally, which will create massive new results for you!

If you take a survey in any workplace or relationship, it's likely that the top item suggested for improvement or change will be communication. Everyone talks about communicating better, but there is very little practical education or instruction on how to effectively grow this skill. We know when communication is not going well. It causes fights, misunderstandings, frustration, poor results, and overall leads to anxiety and dissatisfaction.

Confident communication becomes easier when you are practicing regular confidence-building statements (some may even be about communication!), connecting to your inner guiding wisdom, and having increased clarity about where you are headed!

What is Confident Communication?

Confident Conflict-Free Communication is the skill of being able to say anything you need to say to anyone with 100% complete respect to all those involved in the conversation (including yourself!) This is a skill that when mastered has the potential to unlock amazing new levels of confident living. With this skill there will be less and less wishing you had said something or trying to figure out how to say something and more and more speaking authentically in the moment. Here are a few examples!

- Asking your boss to be paid what you are worth in a way that is heard and considered.
- Approach previously avoided relationship conversations.
- Communicate with your teenager who thinks you are an alien speaking in a foreign language!
- Address "the unspoken obvious" in the room
- Tell your son "No" I cannot babysit for your kids tonight.

It would be impossible to give you this entire skill set in one short chapter, so my goal is to give you a few simple guidelines to help you be aware of when communication is not going well and a few simple steps to begin shifting to more effective communication. Once you have mastered the basics, I have included a few additional resources for deeper learning at the end of this chapter.

What Does Confident Communication Replace?

For years I had two conversations running in my head most of the time: the one I said out loud that I thought would "please people" and "keep the peace" and the genuine authentic thoughts that were happening inside that I did not feel free to speak. Here are some common communication patterns that exist:

- Fight - we go into defense mode and fight to prove our perspective is "right"
- Flight - we avoid or run from conversations. Walking on eggshells is a version of flight as it is avoiding necessary conversation that we fear may upset another person
- Freeze - we want to say something, but the words just don't come out.
- Faint - avoid the conversation through any means, sickness, absence, etc.
- Fawn - saying whatever you feel will please the other person and keep the peace.

(I refer to these as the 5 Fs of emotional trauma. For a more detailed explanation of them listen to Episode #2 of the Becoming Unsilenced Podcast.)

Effective communication must include several elements:
1. Safety
2. Taking responsibility for self
3. Openness to listening to others' perspectives
4. Valuing relationships over being "right"

When these four elements are present in one person's communication, it opens the door and invites others into the conversation in new ways. To restate that, it is not a requirement for the other person in a conversation to desire change. You drive change through your own behavior.

Here are some signs that those 4 elements of safety are not present. Check the boxes next to these signs to see how many you have experienced in the last week.
- ☐ Talks over you
- ☐ Does not show respect
- ☐ Does not listen for understanding

- ☐ Makes no attempt to understand your viewpoint
- ☐ Avoids important conversation
- ☐ Interrupts
- ☐ Shames you for your thoughts/ideas ("That's such a dumb idea. Where did you come up with that?")
- ☐ Dismisses or devalues your opinion without consideration
- ☐ Tells you how things will be or should be
- ☐ Yells/shouts
- ☐ Blames by using "You" statements ("You made me ___.")
- ☐ Feels dangerous to speak authentically for fear that the other person will be angry/violent or attack verbally
- ☐ There is a pattern of lying and dishonesty in communication
- ☐ Makes you feel "crazy" ("I didn't really say that. You are making that up." This is a significant warning of narcissistic behavior.)
- ☐ Jealous
- ☐ Isolating
- ☐ Doesn't want to solve problems and/or doesn't feel like talking about it now and offers no promise of when such a conversation could take place.

If you have check marked more than 3 of these it is a strong indicator that there are unhealthy communication patterns happening in your relationships. Any check marks at all may be a warning sign of toxic communication patterns. This resource does not address extreme toxic communication; however, if you resonate with this list strongly, please reach out to me or another coach, counselor or therapist to support you in understanding and changing toxic relationship patterns.

Here is a set of characteristics to help you understand what emotionally healthy conversations look like:
- ☐ Others listen to what you have to say
- ☐ Curious
- ☐ Asks questions
- ☐ Open to seeing your new perspective and viewpoint
- ☐ Co-creates solutions
- ☐ Respects your ideas, thoughts, and feelings
- ☐ Gives you space to talk
- ☐ Values your insights
- ☐ Asks for clarification
- ☐ Speaks in a calm voice
- ☐ Takes ownership

- ☐ Uses "I" statements (I felt uncomfortable when XYZ happened.)
- ☐ Unconditional acceptance/safety
- ☐ Shares the truth in a loving way
- ☐ Asks for thoughts of others
- ☐ Firm
- ☐ Confident

Take a moment to review the healthy communication list. Checkmark all that you see in your existing relationships, whether at home or work.

Daily Practice – How to Improve your Communication

Let's take a look at the nuts and bolts of how to begin improving your communication! Depending on where you are at on your own communication journey these 4 practices may stretch you a little - or a LOT! - so it's important to have compassion for yourself in the process (see Key Practice 5!) and to give yourself permission to take one step at a time. When communication does not go well, consider it feed-forward information instead of failure. Feed-forward is a word that refers to gathering information for the purpose of using that information to adjust in the future. Get curious about what worked and about what didn't work, and you will find clues on how to adjust your communication.

It's important to note that we are not attempting to change how others communicate. We are only taking responsibility for our own communication. The only person you can control is you so don't waste any energy and effort attempting to change or control someone else's behavior. What I expect you will see -- as I have time and time again -- is that when you take responsibility for and change your own behavior, others choose to change theirs willingly. Or they find a way to exit themselves out of your life. Let's explore the 4 requirements for effective communication in more detail.

Safety

The most important element that has to be in place for healthy communication is safety. Now, you may expect me to say safety between the people communicating - and yes that is important - but there is one area of safety that goes much deeper.

Internal safety is key. Do you trust yourself enough to keep yourself safe in any situation? Often, we blame other people for causing us not to feel safe, but the true root of safety is internal. Internal safety comes from trusting yourself completely, knowing you have your own back, and trusting yourself to make the best choices for your optimal emotional, mental and physical health. When you begin a conversation from a space of internal safety, communication is already transforming.

The #1 most important focus for anyone desiring to improve communication is to get to know themselves better in order to deepen self-trust. This is what keys 1, 2, and 3 have been all about! The more you master all five keys your confidence level will continue to grow; as it grows, your communication will improve.

The second necessary requirement for safety is safety among those who are communicating. Emotional, mental, and physical safety. If there is fear in any way, it shuts down open productive communication. How do you know when a conversation has moved outside the zone of safety? Refer back to the checklist of unhealthy communication patterns. If any of these behaviors happen, safety is not present in the communication, and it is a red flag signal to pause the conversation and focus on restoring safety. No authentic and effective communication can occur when safety is absent.

A quick note to emphasize if you have a person or people in your life that insist on toxic communication patterns: love and respect yourself enough to minimize or eliminate connection with them. You are worthy and deserving of respectful healthy communication. Also, know that as your confidence grows and you shift your behaviors it may invite the other person to change but the choice is their responsibility. At times toxic patterns are so ingrained that it's better to remove yourself from the conversations.

Healing your own internal triggers is a significant part of communicating confidently. I'll address this more in a future book, but here it is important to know that anytime another's words, actions, or lack thereof generate an emotional response from you, it is a signal that a sore, unhealed spot in your soul has been touched. This is another opportunity to work with a coach, therapist, or counselor to further your complete emotional healing.

Here I'll provide you with some specific language you can use as you become more self-aware about safety in communication.

- It seems that we are not making progress in this conversation right now. Let's pause and resume it when we can be respectful and take responsibility for ourselves.
- (Someone shouting at you) I'll be happy to resume this conversation when we can both speak calmly and rationally. For now, I'm going to pause it. (Walk away, hang up, drive away)
- (Asking for Safety) When _____ happens in our conversation it makes me feel unsafe. I'll be happy to continue when we can speak respectfully and each take responsibility for our part of the conversation.

- (Blame: When anyone casts blame there is no safety in the conversation.) I can see that you feel like what has happened is my fault. I'd like to understand more about that and share more of my perspective. Are you open to continuing the conversation in that direction, or shall we continue this conversation at a time when we are both ready to speak openly and transparently?
- (Distracted/not listening) It feels like I don't have your full attention right now. When is a better time that we could talk without distractions?

*A note on distracted conversations. Our cell phones take up a lot of our mental energy and attention today. A best practice when communicating is to silence your cell phone and put it somewhere where you physically cannot see it. I remember the day I began doing this with my daughter. Each time I engaged with her I put the cell phone away and turned and looked directly at her. I was shocked to discover how many of our conversations I had with one eye and ear on my cell phone. One day she said, "why are you just looking at me while we talk?" and I had the opportunity to say, "our conversations are so important to me that I've decided to put away my phone completely while we talk." I also realized she had been asking me to do this in her own way for a long time by telling me I wasn't listening to her. (My response always was, "I'm listening, I'm just checking this one last text/email/project," while sending the message that she was less important than the text/email/project.)

Safety and self-awareness go hand in hand. Begin to notice what is happening in your body during a conversation. What physical feelings are you having? What emotional feelings are you having? Physical and emotional responses are all clues to your level of safety -- internally and externally.

Taking Responsibility for Self

One of my favorite humorous quotes is "Not my circus, not my monkey." I'd invite you to take an inventory of your daily conversations and ask yourself how many of your conversations are about someone else's "monkey/business.". How many times are you tempted to tell someone what to do with or how to fix their "monkey"? This includes your family members, adult kids, co-workers, and boss. It's easy to think we have a "right" to give input on how other people handle their business. The truth is we can respect others enough to trust they have enough wisdom to take care of their problems in a way that's best for them.

Communication becomes focused and effective when we get laser clear

about what is and what is not our responsibility. Here are some indications you might be tending someone else's monkey:
- Giving advice (without being asked)
- Telling someone what they "should" do differently
- Telling someone what they did "wrong"
- Telling another person what so-and-so said about them
- Telling someone they "made you feel ___." (No one can "make" you feel anything. Your feeling is the response you choose to a situation.)

Judging and criticizing others is a dangerous space and is ALWAYS getting involved in someone else's "monkey/business." Judgment and criticism really are saying that my perspective of how you should behave is the "right" one and unless you live up to my exact idea of "right" I'm not going to be happy with you. But here is the thing: How did your perspective become the "right" one and the measurement for how others should behave? Isn't your perspective of what is right and wrong a mixture of what your parents, teachers, and religion taught you? So, what makes your perspective better than the next person's whose perspective and behavior are also a result of their collective conditioning?

Taking responsibility in communication also means allowing others to take on responsibility for themselves. Respect that they are the expert on themselves, and each individual has the right to choose their own behavior and response. You do not need to fix, help, hint, suggest, or be silent. If you have something to say you can own your perspective and communicate it clearly as your own perspective and not as a standard of right/wrong for others.

Take a look at the check list of unhelpful behaviors earlier in this chapter. How many of these have you done to others in the last week? You can begin taking responsibility now by using the following confidence-building statement: "I take responsibility for my communication."

Challenge: Create a confidence-building statement that reflects your commitment to communicate healthily 100% of the time.

Openness to Listen for Another's Perspective - Curiosity

The opposite of judgment and criticism are openness and curiosity. Openness and curiosity are fundamental skills for taking personal responsibility. When you take ownership of your own behavior it allows one to become curious and open about what drives the behavior of others. Cultivating openness and curiosity in communication creates space for magic in conversation.

Curiosity replaces presuming we know why others say, act, and do what they do. Often, we respond to others based on a story we have created in our head about them or the situation instead of pausing to be genuinely curious about their perspective. Create a new habit of asking curious questions without being attached to the answer. Genuine openness and curiosity help the other person in a conversation to feel listened to and heard.

Conflict occurs when people do not feel seen, heard, or understood. When understanding happens, new pathways open up and new results happen solely based on a new shared understanding. How do you cultivate curiosity and openness?

Open-ended questions are the best way to demonstrate curiosity. Practice asking questions without attachment (judgment) to what answer is given. Curious questions are open-ended and invite a response other than yes or no. Quality open-ended questions also do not contain your own opinion and show genuine interest in the other person's perspective. Here are some examples:

- How did you reach that conclusion?
- I noticed your voice raised and you sounded frustrated just now - what's that about?
- Help me understand how you arrived at this solution?
- Would you tell me more about that?
- Where did you learn that?
- Is that your own belief or did someone else teach you that?
- What's not working for you here?
- What is working for you here?
- What would your ideal solution to this problem be?
- Can you see a perspective I may not have considered?
- Where did you first learn that idea/belief?

Genuinely valuing another person's thoughts, ideas, and perspective and truly listening builds volumes of safety and credibility in conversations. This is especially true when the person you are communicating with feels like they can say whatever they need to say without an emotional response, defensive communication or judgment.

In my experience as a coach, it can take at least 3 questions to get to the true essence of another person's thoughts and feelings. Be willing and patient to listen to a response, and instead of giving your opinion of the response, ask another curious question. Be aware of crafting your own response in your head instead of fully listening to the response from the other person.

Valuing Relationships Over Being "Right"

Wayne Dyer is one of my most treasured mentors on the personal growth path. His books, talks, and energy continue to make an impact long after he has departed from his physical body. It was through Wayne Dyer that I first encountered the idea that "it's more important to be happy than right."

At the heart of the statement is this: valuing strong healthy relationships is far more important than needing to get our own way. This also does NOT mean that you keep your own thoughts and opinions silent to keep peace with others (that's not safety in communication) or that you devalue your own preference in deference to others.

What it does mean is valuing the discovery of common ground and highest purpose for all in communication becomes the priority. This approach creates space to value the unique perspective of everyone in the conversation.

My son and I both have strong opinions about business and marketing. As an entrepreneur, I learned and engaged in different marketing practices than he was being taught at the university. Each time we discussed my business marketing strategy it ended in frustration for both of us. He was wanting me to see the "textbook" way to do things and I was wanting him to "acknowledge" my real-life wisdom and experience.

After one particularly heated conversation where we stepped out of the "safety" zone, I had to take a hard look at my behavior and take responsibility for it. I was asking him for advice from what he was learning, and then getting mad at him for giving me said advice! It was then that we both realized that we had two different perspectives that didn't match -- and that was okay. We agreed that we valued our relationships with each other far more than any marketing strategy, so we agreed not to discuss marketing strategy for a while. We are already back to discussing marketing strategy, but we are each taking responsibility for our part in the communication. We are more open and curious to each other's perspective.

Let's practice choosing the highest common goal in relationships instead of getting stuck in the details and the "rightness or wrongness" of things that really won't matter 20 years from now. Forcing your perspective on details causes fractures in relationships that take years or lifetimes to repair. It's just simply not worth it. I'd much rather have a happy, healthy, thriving relationship with my son than be "right" about my marketing strategy!

New Perspective = New Results

Confident conflict-free communication only requires that YOU be willing to change how you communicate. This role model's communication to others in a new way and invites new responses from them. Be firm in your commitment to communicate according to the healthy communication list instead of the unhealthy list. As you practice the new way of communicating, new results will come. Those new results will decrease your self-doubt and increase your self-confidence.

It takes courage to change! I felt sick to my stomach for two days before and after my first conversation where I applied these guidelines. It was such a different way to communicate than what I had known. It's direct, confident and upfront instead of passive, avoiding and unclear. I was proud of myself for making it through that first conversation. Now, 11 years later, I confidently speak in this manner a majority of the time. I can confidently say anything that needs to be said with complete respect to myself and the people around me.

However, it is important to note at this point that if a person does not have any interest in safe communication or taking responsibility for their own behavior, consider the possibility that it's time to part ways and invite people into your life who are willing to communicate in healthy ways. Love yourself enough to let go of those who prefer toxic communication styles and find those who thrive on emotionally healthy relationships.

There are few things that help life flow more smoothly than high-quality communication. Mastering the art of communicating unlocks doors and relationships that previously remained mysteriously locked. It can increase your effectiveness (and your income) at work and act like oil for rusty gears in your personal relationships. Most importantly, when you trust that you have the ability to communicate anything to anyone your confidence skyrockets!

Bonus: Communication strategy for leaders (boss, supervisor, parent)

Let's add one more skill to our communication toolkit. Leaders have a unique role that requires accountability to action. Let's look at a conversation outline that can be used for leaders in any position, whether parent, teacher, supervisor or executive.

1. I noticed that (insert an observed fact here while avoiding your opinion, i.e., you didn't take out the trash, finish your homework, complete the assigned task).
2. Tell me about that? What happened? (Be Curious)
3. Great, thanks for helping me understand. In the future can we

agree that (insert required action, e.g., trash will be taken out by 9 pm, homework will be completed on time, job tasks will be completed thoroughly)?
4. So that we are clear -- are we in agreement that (state defined action and timeline)?
5. Fist bump/high five -- thanks for your commitment to getting this done. I appreciate it.

Follow-up conversation when the outcome is met.
- Hey Bill, I noticed that you completed (stated action in defined time) and you really did awesomely! Thanks so much. I really appreciate that! (Insert a genuine statement about how the completed action benefits you or others.) It's so nice to come home to a clean kitchen and no trash piled up!

Follow-up conversation when the outcome is not met:
1) Hey Bill, I noticed that (XYZ) did not get completed.
2) What happened?
3) Okay, great. I understand and thank you for sharing but that does not change the fact that (XYZ) needs to be completed on time.
4) What is your plan to correct the situation and get it done?
5) Great, thanks. Let's just be clear that if it is not done by (timeframe) that (consequence) will happen.

Stories of Learning Confident Communication

Klarinda, from Nebraska, began coaching with me when she realized her marriage was toxic and no longer safe for her. In fact, this was her second time marrying the same guy. The relationship was marred by alcoholism, narcissistic behavior, homelessness and even losing custody of her kids at one point.

She came to me for help rebuilding her confidence so she could create a new life. She dived into the five key confidence-building practices with eagerness. I saw her gradually opening up to new levels of confidence as she practiced each key.

For a time, she struggled to embrace new ways of communicating. She was afraid of upsetting her children (now young adults) and dealing with residual guilt from the past. She began to clearly see that if she wanted to have any hope of breaking the generational cycles of codependency, she had to change how she was interacting with her children.

Slowly, she began to hold firm to her boundaries, learned to listen more deeply to what they were saying, and began to understand how unproductive it was to communicate when safety was no longer present in a conversation.

Conversation by conversation, a shift happened. Then, with her confidence growing and restored, one day she met a new gentleman and is happily engaged and living in another state. She credits her new ability to confidently communicate for opening up unlimited possibilities for her, which included welcoming in a new loving partner.

She has a deep heart of compassion for other women in similar situations. If you resonate with her story, her word of advice is to decide that you are not going to tolerate misery and unhappiness any longer. You deserve better. Once you have decided that, find the coach, group, or resources to help you change your life.

There are so many stories I could share here. This has been a life-changing skill! But one of my favorite stories about the change is one that you may identify with: being underpaid in a job that is expecting a high level of performance.

I fell "by accident" into the waste industry. Really it was by exact universal design, but it felt like an accident at that time. I quickly became the first and only female district manager in about a 10-state area. I also entered the industry with no experience at all in the trash business. I realize today that being a woman manager with zero experience, I had about a statistically ZERO percent chance to have been hired in this job under normal circumstances. Yet the universe decided I needed to be there and arranged a set of circumstances that presented me as the ideal candidate for the job! Three years later, I had turned around a failing company and led the team to become a success story. Safety rates were low, profit was at an all-time high, team culture was solid, and underperformers had left and been replaced with higher expectations.

Yet, I was being paid a salary significantly lower than my male peers. I could have shifted into a blaming, complaining, negative attitude over this, but I didn't. It was in these very years I had been practicing my confidence-building statements, connecting with my own value and worth, gaining clarity on what I wanted, and learning new communication skills. I had clarity that I wanted to be paid a fair wage for fair work. I also now had the confidence and skillset to ask for that. I did not demand; instead, I was patient. I looked for opportunities to add more value and then I asked to be paid for it. This happened several times and each time I was granted the increase. On one occasion it was apparent that the company realized just how out of whack my wages were and granted a significant adjustment.

I resigned from the industry being paid a fair wage. I'm confident that had I not known and understood my own value and worth and developed the skillset to ask to be compensated fairly, the company would have been slow to correct the issue on its own.

Resources for Further Learning on Confident Communication:

- Non-Violent Communication: A Language of Compassion by Author Marshall Rosenberg
- Crucial Conversations: Tools for Talking When the Stakes are High by authors Patterson, Grenny, McMillan, and Switzler

CHAPTER 6 - GIVE YOURSELF A BREAK

"Kindness and Compassion give rise to self-confidence, which in turn empowers us to be honest, truthful, and transparent."
— *Dali Lama*

"When we are mindful of our struggles, and respond to ourselves with compassion, kindness, and support in times of difficulty, things start to change."
— *Kristin Neff*

Key Practice 5 - Compassion

What is Compassion?

We have made it to the final confidence-building key! What changes have you already noticed as you practice the previous 4 keys? Change begins little by little and then gains momentum as new practices shift into comfortable daily practices. Key Practice 5 supports the other four keys and acts as the grease in the gears for the other four practices, determining how easily or slowly the practices are implemented.

Compassion acts as the warm blanket of grace that gives us permission to screw it all up and start over again tomorrow without needing to beat ourselves up or feel guilty about it. This is the space where we begin to realize that we don't have to be "perfect." In fact, perfect is an ideal that means something different in the eyes of each individual and therefore becomes an impossible standard to hit.

Instead, it's a place we begin to show ourselves the same love, grace, and gratitude that is easier to extend to everyone else. Return to the image of the newborn baby from chapter 1. Think about the amount of love and grace you would naturally extend to that tiny helpless human. You would be concerned if the baby got hurt, cried or was hungry. You would tend to its every need without judging the fact that it had needs or could not take care of itself.

This is the space of compassion: believing that we each have value and worth, even when we cannot "do" or contribute to the level of self-expectation. You are worthy and deserving of love and grace because you live and breathe and exist! It's not something you have to earn.

What Does Compassion Replace?

Compassion replaces judgment of self and others. Judgment has become such an embedded and engrained way of life that it's not visible until we begin peeling back the layers. Have you caught yourself having high expectations of yourself and others? The space between expectation and reality is judgment. Do you feel like you may never be "enough"? In between the notion of what "enough" may look like, and reality lies judgment. Do you beat yourself up with guilt and belittle yourself when you mess up? That, too, stems from judgment, my friend. Maybe you feel like you are so screwed up from your past and present that it's not possible for you to have happiness -- it's possible for everyone else -- but not you. That is judgment.

Judgment shows up in infinite ways as we act like our opinions of ourselves, and others are gospel truth and law written in stone. Judgment says that, according to the way I have been conditioned to believe, this thought, idea, or action is wrong/bad/unjust.

It's only when we begin to see judgment as an illusion instead of the reality that progress happens, and compassion enters. When we call judgment what it is -- a conditioned response, an illusion -- it's easier to let it go and extend ourselves the grace to be okay no matter the circumstances at any moment.

Our perspective of "right" comes from our layers of conditioning. Believing strongly in the myth of right versus wrong creates judgment. The more you return to love and connection with your pure authentic self, the sillier strong notions of right and wrong become. They are just someone's perspective at a particular point in time. Here we find grace and compassion. Judgment and compassion cannot exist in the same space. We begin to discover that we are all really doing the best we can at any given point in time. When we know better, we do better.

Here's another key insight for you to ponder: Hurt people hurt people. Healing people heal people. When a person acts, speaks, and responds from core hurt, self-doubt or wounding they will perpetuate that same hurt onto others, creating a generational cycle of pain until one person becomes conscious enough to stop the cycle.

When the pain of remaining the same becomes greater than the pain of change, then healing begins. The beautiful thing is that healing people heal people. When you begin using the five key practices and allowing them to change you, it will be noticeable to those around you. Now you are providing an example and role modeling a new way.

In the space where healing occurs, there is a great need for compassion and the release of self-judgment.

Daily Practice -How to Develop Compassion

Cultivating compassion is a daily practice. It's a habit you can develop no matter your current level of compassion. You can begin with these simple easy practices:
1) Ask yourself: what judgments about myself or others have I noticed in the last hour? Recognize the judgment and release it back to the universe.

Example: "Wow, I didn't get anything at all done today. I really don't use my time wisely."

Exploration: Is it really true that you didn't get ANYTHING accomplished? Adding the judgment about time is of no value or benefit. In the present moment you have a choice: do you want to do something different? If so, choose a different action; if not, let the conditioned response of judgment go.

2) Gratitude: Oprah championed the gratitude journal years ago. She openly shares how the power of gratitude transformed her life. The practice of gratitude is a practice of paying attention to life and noticing the beauty and synchronicity around you. Even on the darkest, coldest night, there is a lamp and warm blanket to be grateful for. It's not about repeating empty or meaningless platitudes. It's the practice of noticing the world around you and finding what gives you joy -- and recognizing THAT is gratitude.

Daily practice: Create a daily practice of observing at least three things to be grateful for. Shift your eye to look for what is right, instead of what is wrong. Train it to see the beauty in the world. Even in the deepest sorrow, gratitude exists.

Advanced Practice: Meta or Loving Kindness meditation is an extremely effective compassion practice. For several years I released judgments daily and leaned into gratitude. Then I came to a time in my life where things moved slower than I was comfortable with and my need for self-compassion grew to a new level. During this time, I found several guided Meta/ Loving Kindness meditations that brought me deep peace and self-love.

Meta meditation is all about giving yourself love and kindness, then sharing it with those you love, those you don't love, and the world as a whole. It's a powerful practice. If you would like an additional resource to explore, consider checking out the book "The Joy of Living" by Mingyur Rinpoche.

New Perspective = New Results

Compassion acts as the release valve for all the tension, wounds, could haves, and should haves that build up over the years of our lives. It's the gift to yourself that says, "You are ok. Everything is ok, exactly as it is." Releasing the need to be anything or anyone other than what you are in this moment is liberation!

Compassion softens us and gentles our souls. Energy invested into compassion generates ongoing benefits. Judgment stops us in our tracks. Compassion opens us up and makes us kinder, more caring human beings.

Compassion moves us beyond resistance through acceptance. Dropping the resistance to what is and accepting that everything is as it needs to be in this very moment brings deep joy, peace and freedom. It creates an openness and willingness to let things unfold as the universe intended without exerting the effort of controlling. It's time to stop holding your breath and waiting for the other shoe to drop; it's time to live deeply in the moment through compassion.

Compassion is the salve that comforts our soul. Learning and embracing self-compassion is key on the journey of life mastery and enlightened living. It's often a quality that comes as a result of a universal wake-up call!

The universe has a way of getting our attention one way or another. It's easy to ignore small alerts in our workaholic culture, but when it's time for us to learn this lesson, life circumstances often become so intense that we no longer can ignore the wake-up call.

This is what happened to my dear friend Silvia. She heard some gentle internal knocks that it was time to change some things in her life, yet she was busy as a single parent going to school, working, and being the best mom, she could be. That consumed all her attention, leaving little energy left to explore the gentle knocks.

I share her story here, with her permission. In her case, life gave her no option but to pay attention to the knock on the door for change. It brought her to a radical halt when her kidneys shut down almost overnight. She chose to use this unexpected circumstance as an opportunity to regain deep inner confidence using these five key practices. She has since found a deep peace and trust in life that may have taken her many more years to discover had she not had the opportunity to come to a halt and listen to what the universe was telling her.

Stories of Compassion

Silvia and I met in small town Nebraska working in the concession stands under the Friday night lights of our local high school football game. Our daughters were both in school together and somehow, we made it several years living in the same small community without ever meeting each other. That night, while serving popcorn and hot chocolate at the concession stand, we immediately gravitated toward each other. She is of Mexican nationality and a fluent Spanish speaker. Our spirits recognized each other and soon she became my Spanish mentor, helping me to improve my Spanish language skills.

During the year ahead, we could not have imagined the beautiful, connected friendship that would unfold as we walked circles around the local park speaking in Spanish until my head felt ready to explode. We became fast friends, feeling like we had always been part of each other's lives.

One evening after several weeks apart, Silvia shared that she had been sick all week. Even though my day was full I felt that I needed to go see her. I followed that intuitive nudge (because I live key 2 daily!) and I went to her house, even though it was 10:30 at night. When she opened the door, I instantly sensed something was wrong.

The next few days ahead would reveal that her kidneys had decided to shut down. A rare auto-immune disease kicked in and overnight her kidneys lost 100% of their function. Through a whirlwind of sickness and healthcare decisions, she ended up back in Mexico navigating a new life of dialysis and finding a life-saving donor.

Overnight, Silvia's life was turned upside down. She had to stop all normal activities -- work, school, and her dreams of owning a business -- and learn an entirely new way of being that included dialysis and managing her diet. In the dark days ahead, she would have the opportunity to use all 5 confidence-building keys in the most challenging of times. Thought by thought she created new confidence-building statements. These new confidence-building statements released old limiting beliefs and fears. Then, she slowly began to listen to her own inner guidance instead of the voices of family, friends, and doctors that all seemed to say conflicting things. The key milestone of clarity came moment by moment as she chose acceptance and being 100% present. I watched her spirit begin to soar and was often amazed at her resilience. Through mindfulness and being 100% accepting of her reality -- and choosing to be happy anyway -- she gained complete clarity of each next step forward. That step-by-step clarity guided her to connect with a life-saving donor and as I write this the transplant is soon to be scheduled.

This acceptance and clarity led to a change in how Silvia communicated. I watched her gain her voice advocating for herself, have difficult conversations with her teenage daughter, balance intense conversations with other family members, and have honest, authentic conversations with her friend who emerged to volunteer as her donor. In each conversation, she learned how to create emotional safety, speak clearly, listen more deeply, and find the space of the highest good for all involved.

Silvia embraced each of these confidence-building keys with the greatest amount of self-compassion. Self-compassion is the "grease" that helps you to walk through all of the other steps with grace and ease. Some days she easily embodied all of these keys and other days she hid under her blanket at dialysis while we chatted and hoped for better days. Self-compassion is the acceptance that with ups there will be downs, with health there will sometimes be sickness, with great relationships there will sometimes be conflict. When you embrace self-compassion, you embrace the concept that these highs and lows don't impact your worth or value.

    The depth of the changes we are willing to accept in life determines the depth of transformation that will happen. I saved Silvia's story for last because it exemplifies all of the five key practices. I'm so grateful to be part of her story and that I got to be one of the guides on her literally life-changing transformation. Our human nature fears the darkest night of the soul, yet our divine spirit knows those dark nights will be the very thing that frees us to experience the greatest joy and peace imaginable.

CHAPTER 7 - LIVING THE 5 KEY PRACTICES: LIVING LIFE TO THE FULLEST

"Our deepest fear is not that we are inadequate. Our deepest fear is that we are powerful beyond measure. It is our light, not our darkness that most frightens us. We ask ourselves, 'Who am I to be brilliant, gorgeous, talented, fabulous?' Actually, who are you not to be? You are a child of God. Your playing small does not serve the world. There is nothing enlightened about shrinking so that other people won't feel insecure around you. We are all meant to shine, as children do. We were born to make manifest the glory of God that is within us. It's not just in some of us; it's in everyone. And as we let our own light shine, we unconsciously give other people permission to do the same. As we are liberated from our own fear, our presence automatically liberates others."

— Marianne Williamson, <u>A Return to Love: Reflections on the Principles of "A Course in Miracles"</u>

The 5 Confidence-Building Key Practices: Adapt and Support You as You Grow

You now hold in your possession and knowledge the five key skills that will help you release self-doubt and embrace new levels of confidence every day. These five practices are skills, not one-time fixes. They are skills to be applied as you propel yourself to new levels of confidence and joy on your journey.

Self-doubt is a core characteristic of our human egoic nature. As you operate more from the heart and less from the mind and ego by using these skills, the attention and power you give self-doubt decreases over time. You will begin to quickly recognize the characteristics of self-doubt and see them as a reminder to shift back into your confidence-building skillset.

Today, I have complete confidence in so many skills around which I previously felt tremendous self-doubt. Yet, each time I spiral to a new level of relationship and achievement, new self-doubts emerge and give me the opportunity to explore and move through them. Think of it as a video game where new versions of the same challenge are present on each increasing level. Just as in a video game your skill, agility, and speed of recognizing the obstacle and moving through it increases with each new upward spiral.

These keys are most effective when you use them as a daily practice. Weave them into the fabric of your daily life and soon you will be using them automatically. Now is a good time to remind you that it's estimated to take 7 positives to offset one negative and significant time and repetition to create new strong neural pathways in the brain. At first, it's going to take some effort and intention to turn these keys into a new way of life. Yet, as you balance the old with the new and then make the new your dominant way of life, momentum builds on your confidence journey.

Consider what a thriving life looks like

I find it sad that the majority of people are willing to settle for a life where they simply tolerate much of their existence. I'm here to tell you that you can have it all, you truly can have a thriving life on every level. It just takes a willingness to keep releasing the doubt and embracing the beautiful spirit that you have always been.

Twelve years ago, everything in my world felt chaotic. From that chaos, two commitments to myself emerged. 1) I am not willing to live the next 20 years of my life as miserable as the last 20, and 2) I was determined to find a way to break generational cycles for my kids.

The universe gifted me these 5 confidence-building keys as the foundation of my new life. I'm forever grateful because they completely changed my life. In future books, I'll share additional key skills that build on this foundation, such as how to completely heal the past, how to break generational cycles and patterns for good, the seven levels of confident living, and more.

Along the path, I began to imagine the beautiful life that would fulfill me at every level. I asked myself, "what would it look like to live a thriving life in all areas?" Each day I took steps in a direction to create that reality. Here's what I understand now: this was the vision the universe had for me all along! I was just tuning into it! It's a beautiful thing to tune into all that the universe has to offer; to surrender completely and begin to receive what one is truly worthy and deserving of.

My body and soul thrive on warm weather and sun, so the cold harsh winters of Nebraska literally felt like they sucked my soul out of me. As I embraced what my thriving level 10 life would look like, one key piece of that was living in a warmer climate during the winter seasons. I also longed to live in a place where I could easily connect with like-minded people. I also love coffee shops and living in a place where I can walk to everything I need. The universe has abundantly delivered that to me. The entire time spent writing this book I am living in Mazatlán, Mexico in the Central Historic district of the town. This community feeds my soul in so many ways! The warmth, the culture, the language, and the people make me feel at home! One of my favorite confidence-building statements is "this or something better" and certainly the universe has delivered me "something better!" My spirit and soul which used to struggle day and night are now at peace. When an inner conflict arises, I surround it with the greater being of who I am instead of falling for thinking I am the conflict.

I'm incredibly excited to see where your confidence-building journey takes you! Please send me an email at inspire@tslimits.com and let me know how these skills are changing your life moment by moment.

The Journey is Easier with Others

Change can be uncomfortable and lonely. Charting a new path and direction that is different from that of your friends, family and co-workers can feel exciting and challenging. Throughout my own journey plugging into groups of like-minded people committed to their own growth and development was key!

I desired to connect with people who would give me a hand and pull me up and rise to a new level with me. Not people who would pull me back into the confusion and chaos and commiserate with me. I found those connections through exploring new interests, taking classes, and most of all inviting the universe to connect me with them!

One of the most powerful transformative groups I connected with was a small circle of women who chose to meet weekly (virtually) for growth, encouragement and support. Each week we chose to dedicate an hour and we rarely missed that time. Only death or extreme sickness kept us each away. In that space we found a safe place to share tears, joy, lessons learned, and see examples of others actively living confidently.

Traveling with like-spirited individuals determines the speed of your journey. It's easier to not get stuck along the road when you have fellow travelers who stop and help you get back on the path.

Take a moment now to consider who will go on this journey with you. Do you already have intentional travelers you can partner with? If not, take a moment to consider who might be a partner on this journey for you.

Anchor Your Learning

You have just learned life-changing skills. How will you remind yourself each day to choose to use them? In the beginning, change takes a lot of energy and effort to consciously choose to use a new skill instead of an old comfortable habit. Therefore, it's key to have an anchor or a reminder to choose the new skills.

An anchor is something that your brain comes to strongly associate with the new change. It could be a song, a statue on your desk, or an item you wear such as a ring or necklace. Throughout my healing journey, I have used pieces of jewelry as anchors. My first physical anchor was a necklace that had a hot air balloon, an angel wing, and a mantra medallion on it. Each time I touched it I was instantly reminded of why change was so important to me. I'd take a deep breath, shake the nerves out of my stomach, and choose a new action.

Each time I entered a new cycle of growth, I chose a piece of jewelry to represent that phase. A necklace, earrings, a beautiful ring... they went with me everywhere constantly reminding me to choose consciously.

Anchoring your learning to a physical object, a favorite song, or something you wear consistently accelerates changes. You brain automatically strengthens the new neuro pathways each time it sees, hears or experiences the anchor.

WRAP-UP

Now you have the knowledge of the five key confidence-building practices. Knowledge is the first step but is only useful when you convert it into experiential learning. Magic happens when you combine knowledge and experience into a new way of being. How will you take these practices and convert them into experience and become a new, more authentic you? What has self-doubt cost you in your life? It has stolen enough of your future already. You deserve to reclaim your life and confidently live each day.

It takes commitment and sticking to that commitment. That is easier when you do it with others. Give yourself the gift of change. Take a moment now to determine how you will incorporate these key practices daily. I want to leave you with one last thought. I heard this statement from a speaker at a banquet when I was most in need of hearing it. Now I pass it on to you: **You are worth the life you have yet to live.** And you deserve to live that life with confidence in every moment.

www.ingramcontent.com/pod-product-compliance
Lightning Source LLC
Chambersburg PA
CBHW070306220526
45465CB00004B/1762